Fate
By
Alex Phillips Hawkes

I'd like to formally dedicate this book to those who held my hand and pushed me forward when I thought I couldn't go any further.

*To my best friend, to my family.
I love you all and you all are the reason this became a reality.*

FATE

Copyright © 2024 by Alex P Hawkes

The following novella is a work of fiction. Any Resemblance to any person, alive or dead, is purely a coincidence. All characters and settings are a product of the author's imagination.

ISBN: *9798858852988*

All rights reserved. No part of these works can be reproduced, scanned, rewritten or translated in any form, digital or traditional, without permission from the author

alexphillipshawkes@gmail.com

Imprint: Independently published

Ash's Playlist:

- Crush culture - Conan Gray
- People watching - Conan Gray
- (Un)lost - The Maine
- Lonely dance - Set It Off
- This is home - Cavetown
- Love Love Love - Of Monsters and Men
- Movies - Conan Gray
- Boys Will Be Bugs - Cavetown
- Lemon boy - Cavetown
- Gilded Lily - Cults
- My R - Lollia
- You're on your own kid - Taylor Swift
- Lonely Ones - LOVA
- Teen Idle - MARINA
- Why am I like this? - Orla Gartland
- My own person - Ezra Williams
- Serotonin - Acoustic - Tom walker
- Born without a heart - Faouzia
- Family Line - Conan Gray
- Seventeen - MARINA
- Cardigan - Taylor Swift
- Softcore - The Neighbourhood
- Cake - Melanie Martinez
- Comfort crowd - Conan Gray
- If we have each other - Alec Benjamin
- Midnight love - Girl in red

- *I need to be alone - Girl in red*
- *Wrecking ball - Mother Mother*
- *Anti-hero - Taylor Swift*
- *All i wanted - Paramore*
- *Karma - Taylor Swift*
- *Delicate - Taylor Swift*
- *Rue - Girl in red*
- *This is me trying - Taylor Swift*
- *Older - Sasha Alex Sloan*
- *Human - Christina Perri*
- *Blame it on the kids - AViVA*
- *Margorie - Taylor Swift*
- *The family jewels - MARINA*
- *Not really a friend - Rosa*
- *Angry - Paravi*
- *Man's world - MARINA*
- *Vampire - Olivia Rodrigo*
- *Born to die - Lana Del Ray*
- *Mess It up - Gracie Abrams*
- *Falling - Harry Styles*
- *Everything I wanted - Billie Eliish*
- *What was I made for? - Billie Eilish*
- *Closure - Taylor Swift*
- *Bigger Person - Lauren Spencer Smith*
- *Miss Wanna Die - JubyPhonic*
- *Parents - YUNGBLUD*
- *The village - Wrabel*

"Trust the magic of new beginnings."

1.
The reason, not the blame.

It's like it all flashed before my eyes; the sound, the light, the pain, the blood, the look on my brother's face... and it was all my fault. I saw my brother's cries and my frozen expression as they announced the time of death, carrying my parents' lifeless bodies into a separate ambulance. I was stuck, I didn't know what to do, what to feel, what to think. My parents were gone, and I don't know how, or why. All I did know was that, somehow, I was the cause, the blame.
And as I turned at the door, I knew that I wanted nothing more than to be the reason. The reason for everyone's safety, for their freedom.

So that's where I find myself sneaking out, a large duffle bag slung over my shoulder, prepared to find people, determined and capable to help me take down who picked me up on one of the worst nights of my life.

"I'm sorry Alex." I whispered when I passed my brother's bed earlier on. "I'll be back for you." I promised. I will be. I'll be back home when my plan is more stable. When I'm more stable...

I let a few tears fall as I started running. Where? I'm not sure. But I know it'll be far. They'll send search parties as soon as they realise I've left. After all, I know their plan, they don't want that getting out I'm sure.

Especially since they aren't even close to being ready.

This run will be long, draining and scary. but it's necessary. I'm doing what's right. And I'd die if it meant saving everyone else.

2.
Racing against the clock

I left at 2am on the friday and ended up in Ventura's capital at 6am on the saturday. And although I stopped off at a local inn for a nap Friday evening, I desperately needed a rest. I decided to wander around the place for some food, thankfully I snatched a fair amount of money so decent food and water shouldnt be too hard to get ahold of, although a roof will be pretty difficult, seeing as I'm only 15. It's not like I can buy my own house.
I take a seat in a local cafe, thank a waitress for my glass of water and pull out my phone. My parents brought me my first phone when I was 9, only because they got fed up with my constant nagging, and I'm very thankful that they did. My phone was confiscated along with my brothers by Miss Wicker the moment we walked through the door, but it wasn't very well hidden and nothing was deleted off of it. So I

scroll through all of my old messages, group chats and my old social media platforms to see if anyone rings any bells.

After scrolling around for a little bit I notice most people have changed or swapped their old accounts. It was easy to find a few people but if I did remember someone it would soon lead to the discovery that they either no longer live in the city or have cut socials to 'romanticise their adventures'. Typical.
But just as I'm about to call it quits and pay for my drink, I stumble upon someone's name that rings multiple bells.

@r_paramorex

"Paramore... where have i heard that before..." I whisper to myself, trying hard to think back into my past. I speed scroll through their following list and almost cry when I find her.

@leilap_xox

Leila... my childhood best friend. the girl I did everything with for as long as I can remember. Our parents were best friends which instantly meant we were too. I begin to tear up as I scroll around her account, reading through the

countless messages we'd sent each other and realise she still lives in the same house she did almost 6 years ago.
But while reading through the messages I noticed some unread ones, ones from 2018, 2019 and 2020. They stop after that.
Some messages were telling me how she missed me, how she needed me, how she wished I didn't leave so soon and others were telling me about her life, what she was up to day to day and how she wished I'd been there with her.
Then I remember. She's under the impression that I'm dead...

The messages stop on the first of october 2019. it was a birthday message, as well as a closure message. This is where I feel my cheeks start to dampen.
I immediately want to message back, to tell her I'm not dead, to tell her I'm only minutes away. but that's only normal in movies. I can't just text her. She'll think she's being trolled, laugh it off and block me. But I can't not say anything.
So I become some character from a murder mystery novel, suck it up and start typing.

"Hey leila... reading your messages has honestly left me in tears. I love you so much.

and maybe this isn't the best way to tell you but... I am in fact alive. I would love to explain everything to you but maybe an online chat isn't the best space to tell you. It's definitely a conversation that needs to be had in person."

And... sent...

My heart rate increases as I see her immediately come online. But it's not until I see the word "typing" show up on my screen that I start to get worried. I guess I need to accept that there isn't any easy way of telling your childhood best friend that you aren't really dead, that you've been alive the entire time but we're way off the grid for 6 years. I just have to tell her...
And it's like what, 2023 now? Surely everyone does everything over messages now.

"OMG I KNEW IT." Was her first reply. It almost makes me laugh. "I haven't stopped worrying about you for years! I'm not even gonna question, I've missed you so much girl!" I screw up my face slightly. "You have to come over right away. I haven't moved anywhere, so I trust the real Ashley will be able to get here without any address." I smile and get up, tipping the waitress generously and am on my

12

way. The walk was pretty easy, once I passed a few landmarks the rest of the path just came to me. I've walked this walk so many times it's almost engraved in my brain.

And although I'm overjoyed to see her again, I'm just as nervous. She's now what, 17? She's probably changed so much! And what am I even going to say? I can't exactly tell her the real reason as to why I've been MIA. What if she decides I'm not good enough anymore? That she's secretly angry at me and is inviting me over just to slam a door in my face? She must have moved on by now, she probably has loads of other friends, friends who were able to be there for her when i wasn't able to be… was I expecting her to just stay the same simple, pain filled little girl I left behind? Of course she won't be. She's grown up and changed, probably fell in and out of love a few times, maybe changed her wardrobe, her likes and dislikes?

Maybe I should have thought this through a little more…

3.
Under pressure

After what felt like the longest walk of my life, I finally made it to the Paramore's household. I forgot for a moment how big this place was. My breath gets caught up in my throat as I walk through the gate, up the hill and take my last step towards the front door. I don't knock right away, I pace back and forth on the patio for a few minutes, you know, to make sure I'm doing the right thing? Then, as I run my fingers through my long, matted hair, my mind wins over my heart and I reach to ring the bell. After a hot second I hear footsteps gradually get louder and louder, see the handle being slowly pushed down and the door creak open.
This is it. The moment of truth.

"Hello? Who are you?" I smile awkwardly as Mrs Paramore's stands straight faced in the doorway. Though, her expression starts to

change. As if she starts to recognise me in slow motion.
"Oh my.. Ashley? Is that you, dear?" The name sends an unexpected shiver down my spine. I nod and move my hair out of my face.
"Hola, Mrs Paramore..." I say with a false sense of bravery. She ushers me in and leads me into the kitchen, asking me loads of questions on the way.

"My dear you must be thirsty, here, have some tea." she almost forces a cup into my hands. I politely thank her but don't drink it. I'm not much of a tea person.
"So tell me, how are you? Where have you been all these years?"
"Well I... I've been-"
"Oh my god! How's that brother of yours? Alex? Right? Where is he?"
"Uh... well he's-"
"Oh that poor boy, he was so sweet, and charming. You both really were spitting images of your parents. In looks and personalities." I shallow a large lump and swish around my drink.
"Ashley, would you like something to eat? Your way skinnier than I remember. Have you been eating plenty?"

"Thank you, but I... I ate before I got here. I'm really not hungry." That was a lie but I want nothing more than to see Leila.
"Oh alright dearie, well Leila is out at the moment, not sure when she'll be back. That girl really lives on her own planet. doesn't care to tell her own mother what she's up to or when she'll be home nowadays." Just as she says this, I hear the front door open and close. A familiar voice calls out to her mom as she passes through the multiple corridors, she happens to pass the kitchen, and as she passes she seems to notice me. She stands frozen in the doorway. I look at her and our eyes lock. I put down my cup and jumped from the stool I was sitting on. Neither of us said anything to break the silence, actually it was her mom who broke it.
"Oh look, there she is." Leila moves her attention onto her mom and gives her a look that seems to say 'don't start now'. I take a step backwards.
"Yeah, I texted you that I was heading back home. Didn't you see it?" She makes it sound like she's unbothered, but I know she's just hiding her annoyance. I fidget with the strings on my hoodie, not exactly sure on what to do.
"Well you know how I am with those apps, all you had to do was ring me, tell me your plans."

She's casually sipping her tea as she talks, as if she's being reasonable.
"Oh sure, I have to call and text multiple times before I get a reply but Rose just has to text once. Alright mom. That's fine."
"I don't like this attitude young lady, you've only just got in the house, and your friend is here." her high pitched, posh voice is screaming with fake innocence, I could hear it from miles away. I can also tell that this probably isn't the way she'd be if there wasn't a guest in the room.
Unfortunately I remember this happening more than I'd like to admit.

"Fine, I'll get out of your hair. Me and Ashley were about to go upstairs anyway." and before another word can be said Leila grabs my wrist, guides me out of the kitchen and up the stairs into her bedroom. As I walk up the stairs I spot pictures on the walls and shelves, some old, some new but one in particular caught my eye. It's a picture of me, Leila, Rose, my brother and my parents. We've all got ice cream or ice lollies in our hands. It was actually taken a day before the accident. I remember it as if it was yesterday. It was after school on Thursday and Mrs Paramore was working late so we all went to the beach until she finished. Everything about that day was perfect… the smells, the sights, the laughs, the-

My thoughts were interrupted as Leila slams shut her bedroom door and apologies on her mothers behalf.

"Anyway.. How are you? Girl, I haven't seen you in years! I bet a lot has happened in that time!" I laughed nervously and took a seat at the bottom of her bed. Thinking still about what I should say and what I shouldn't.
"It's such a long story! Uh- would it be ok if I freshened up a little first? I've been travelling for a while." I smile awkwardly as she sits down next to me. She smiles back as she nods.
"Of course! You know where your room is. Just meet me back down here when you're ready!"

Yes. I have my own room here. That's how often I was here as a kid.

I thank her and make my way up to the third story where my room was. As I push open the door I realise everything is exactly how I left it. As I look around more memories start flowing back. It's amazing what a single room can unlock.

I aim for the bed and collapse on top. My legs are in so much pain right now, I didn't even realise how exhausted I was until now. But I can't just lay here. I have stuff to do.
I pull myself together and rummage through my bag, trying to pick something more... Me? I guess, to change into. All I have is a short sleeved white top and blue ripped jeans, and they aren't a pair that's supposed to be. I desperately need to go shopping.
I quickly change in the bathroom connected to my room, throwing my hoodie, cape and mask away as I do, ready to burn later on. I don't want anything to do with them anymore. I'm not one of them.

When I stand up looking in the direction of the body sized mirror I finally take time to study myself. My long, black, wavy hair is all matted from the wind and the absence of a hair brush, my tanned skin is covered in scars from head to toe, my most noticeable scar being one covering the majority of my right hand and wrist, and my eye...
I immediately put a black glove on my hand and covered my eye with my hair. These things don't need to be revealed today.
But even after these small adjustments I still don't feel right. I still don't feel or look like me...

I sigh and turn away, walking out into my bedroom, when I notice a pair of scissors on my desk. I approached them and looked into the blades, an idea immediately came to mind. I take them into the bathroom, look into the mirror and start cutting my hair, the more of my messy curls I watch hit the floor the more I start to feel like myself. I keep cutting until I recognise my reflection. Now my hair stops just below my chin and the back ends drop a little further. I drop the scissors and just look at it for a minute. I adjust my parting by moving it to the side and just stare.
I feel different. Like what's inside finally matches what's on the outside…

I clean up the bathroom and put everything away then approach the mirror one last time. And for the first time in my life, I know who's staring back at me.

"You've got this.. Ash."

4.
Smiling freely

I exit the bathroom with my head held just a little bit higher. I'm ready now. I've had my doubts but this is the best decision I could've made. I didn't mess this up. I'm more sure of that now. Everyone knows that the best paths in life are the difficult ones.

As I make my way back to Leila I bump into her sister, Rose. She's definitely gotten taller since I last saw her. I almost don't recognise her. She's now got long brown hair with a few light pink streaks in a tidy ponytail. Her makeup is also light, as if it's not there at all and she's wearing a white and dark blue t-shirt, a knee length black skirt plus leggings. Her clothes don't quite fit with the way she looks, in my opinion, But I'm sure it's just a club uniform of some sort. She always liked dancing and gymnastics, maybe it's for that?

"Hey Rose, how are you?" I ask as she looks up from her book. It takes her a minute to reply, maybe due to shock.
"Oh hey Ashley! I'm good thank you, woah- I didn't even recognise you for a moment there- I'm sorry." She pulls me in for a quick hug and closes her book.
"Oh it's ok, don't worry, I get it." I say reassuringly. She then looks down at her watch and her demeanour quickly changes.
"Uh- god I really would love to talk to you but- I'm swamped with extracurricular stuff to do today, I'm so sorry. But it's nice to see you! Especially after- you know- your supposed death. I'll come up and speak to you properly later!" She laughs awkwardly and flies down the stairs, I don't even have a chance to say bye. I shrug it off though. I'm sure there's a simple explanation.

"Right girl you have to tell me every- oh my gosh!" was what Leila said the moment I walked through her bedroom door. She gushes over my new look and swears it fits me so well. It went on for what felt like hours, I just sat and smiled, I guess she still gets distracted easily. She really hasn't changed much at all really.

not on the inside anyway. Physically, she's changed a lot.
Her hair is a lot longer than before and she's clearly had it curled and highlighted, her ears are also pierced which she despised the idea of as a kid, she's also wearing a cropped white T-shirt and light brown cargos which is the last thing i'd expect her to wear. She always used to wear bright colours when we were younger, but looking around her room now, she's clearly started going for a more neutral colour palette now. Which really suits her, I'll admit.

"Right. So. tell me. What has dear Ashley been up to?" she says, looking at me with eager eyes. I look down and pick at my nails in my lap.
"Well… uh- first off, after the accident me and Alex were- uh- we were taken to a children's home. And they didn't allow phones so i couldnt contact anyone… the rule was obviously for safety reasons." I say sliding my phone out of my pocket. This was the best excuse I could come up with and thankfully, she seems to buy it.
"When I left I stole it back from the front desk- they still don't know I have it, or that I left." It's funny because they never used to pay attention to my existence. But I bet they're

running around after me like headless chickens right now.
Her eyes widened and she pretended to drop dead, falling back on her bed.

"Oh my god! I couldn't live without my phone for a day! Let alone 6 years!" she says dramatically. I laugh. Realising how much I missed this. She then sits back up and takes my phone, examining it.
"I did wonder why your phone was so old. Like, look at this thing. We're gonna have to take you shopping to upgrade it right away." I agree and point out how I may need some more clothes. She suggests some great shops we can go to tomorrow. We Immediately dropped the topic of my absence and we just started talking. Talking about nothing in particular, we spoke about everything and nothing at the same time. I was surprised how easy it was. We talked long into the night, at some point I had grabbed out a sleeping bag and stolen a few spare pillows and now we're both staring up at the ceiling.

"Hey Leila..?" I ask in a soft whisper.
"Yeah?"

"Hypothetically... if I was to go by Ash, instead of Ashley... would you call me it?" I hear her sit up then.
"Of course I would, girl!"
"And if I was to.. Change my pronouns? You'd use them too?"
"Of course I- wait!" I sat up myself then, smiling weakly. The moon light creeps through her curtain and lights up her face just enough for me to see her expression change.
"Of course, broski." she says proudly. We burst out laughing and lay back down. She apologies for calling me a girl but I tell her she doesn't need to. Then we start falling asleep.

"Leila?"
"Yeah?"
"I love you."
"I love you too."

I smile, turning on my side and tearing up.

I'd forgotten what this felt like...

5.
Transition time.

I've been staying with the Paramore's for a little over 2 weeks now and every day I've felt more and more free. I'm even being sent to the same school as Rose. Leila used to go there too but dropped out to focus on her dreams, to move away and perfect the 4 main elements. apparently leaving early was the best option to getting a head start, In her words. She didn't really go into too much detail when I asked.
I'll be starting in year 11, Which I'm going to assume will be a lot different from year 5. I only agreed to go because such a high achieving school is a good place to start finding people to help me with this mess of a plan I'm in the middle of creating. I can't save the island all by myself, I need to find people my age who are

capable of the pressure. It can't just be anyone, they need to be relatively powerful too, and ok with fighting. This island is known for its peace after all. People who live here are normally here because they want to run from conflict, not fall into more.
But also school is a good way to keep undercover. No doubt, by now, there are many search parties out looking for me. I need to lay low and watch everything and everyone around me. And a building full of teenagers is a good place to hide and observe.

"Are you excited Ash? I mean, it's school, but you know what I mean." Rose says with an awkward laugh. I smile and look down at my dinner.
"Yeah I am, but you're gonna have to help me. You know, I haven't been to a school in forever!" I joke, putting down my fork.
"You'll be fine, I'm sure of it. You were always good at school before. You're super smart!" Leila chips in, I thank her but am not fully convinced. Now less than a day away from my first day back at school, I'm starting to feel nervous.
I do remember being a little bit of a nerd when I was younger, not overly smart but I would always come home with piles of books and

random facts no one in my family knew. But that was so long ago. I'm different now. I've changed.
And anyway, I haven't been taught anything other than how to strategize and fight for years. I bet I'm way behind on the curriculum.
And also, I don't have any magical powers to 'enhance and transform'. How am I going to learn about magic I don't even have?

"Ash? Do you even know what magic track you're choosing yet?" Rose's question seems to spark more unnecessary panic. so I block it out, shrug it off and it doesn't stick with me for too long. Whatever I choose will have to be an easy one to cheat through. I don't want loads of papers reminding me of my inability to perform magic.
No one on this island over the age of 12 is powerless, and I'm not having that as the reason I go down in the history books. Plus, I'm a spring! A child of one of the most famous families in Ventura! Everyone will expect me to have this incredible never seen before ability but in reality… I don't.

I went to sleep that night completely restless. I've run away, thankfully reunited with my friends, was given a roof over my head and am

now attending school to stay under cover. The easy part of my mission has been completed. Now all I can think about is the many different ways this next part can go terribly wrong. Not only do the people need to be skilled, but they also need to get along, An essential I've recently realised will make the search a lot harder.
And my brother... I need him. But it's too early to go rescue him now, I've only just started walking on my own two feet. I'm not ready. With his help I'd be ready a lot faster, but I just have to do this myself. I know I'm capable.

But I can't help but think... 'What if I fail?'. I could put all this effort in, just to be backstabbed and lose. That outcome has too high a probability. I wish I could shut out this little voice in my head telling me how completely useless this whole thing is, but I can't.
I guess I'm just going to have to see what the universe throws my way. I know I'll be ok.

And just like that, the first day of school came, like a huge ball of light appearing out of thin air.

I wake up at 5 and plan out my day. I've never been to a secondary school before, no doubt they'll do things differently to primary schools. I needed to look over my schedule and memorise the times. I changed into a long sleeve grey t-shirt and black leggings. I should get my proper uniform there. I cover up my eye with my hair again and hide my hand scar with my glove. It's getting harder and harder to hide these things but I have to. there's no way of answering questions you don't even know the answer to.

"Hey Ash? Are you ready to go? We gotta leave soon." I hear Rose say through my closed door. I sigh and open it up.
"Yep, I'm ready." I replied simply. plastering a smile on my face, reaching for my backpack and closing my door behind me.
This is going to be interesting.

We reached the school exactly at 8, I had to get here earlier to get my uniform and check myself in properly. I'd be lying if I said I wasn't completely taken aback by this place. There are people everywhere. Some reading, some playing, some performing magic. It's actually a beautiful sight. Everyones laughing and chatting with each other in their multicoloured uniforms. But not only are there people running around, there are also animals running around

alongside them. That's not what I was expecting. But then I remember guardian animals are gifted to the kids with unique, overpowered magic abilities, and this school is full of those kids. That's probably what they are.
"Welcome to spell bound academy!" Rose announces proudly as we approach what seems to be the main building. This really seems like a magic school out of those fantasy books and shows.
"Now I'll take you to the main office. it's in that side building there. Then I'll drop you off at your first classroom. Do you know what track you're choosing?" every word she said seemed to spill out too fast for me to comprehend. I raise an eyebrow.

"A track? You know, what magic do you do or want to do? Which are you picking? I asked you last night." she says, she seems to notice my blank expression and slows down. "For example, I have invisibility, but I wanted to study emotions. So I am in two different tracks. I'm pretty sure you can do up to 4."
"Oh. cool." I looked down at the ground as we started walking to the office
"I guess I haven't thought about what I wanted to do.." maybe I should have actually looked at

the leaflet I was given when I visited. I probably should have looked over all these 'tracks' and picked one like that. I was too busy worrying about other things that I didn't think to plan this ahead.
"Well they'll give you a list to choose from anyway. oh! here we are!" She pushes open the large oak doors and guides me to the front desk.

"Morning ma'am." she says cooly. I just smile nervously. "I have a new student here. Ash spring!" I wave and walk up next to Rose. The office lady adjusts her glasses and looks at me for a minute. Then starts typing on her computer.
"Ah yes, welcome Miss spring. I'll get you a uniform in a moment, I need you to first tell me what magic ability you have dear." I freeze, swallowing hard. What should I say? I don't even think I'll ever have a- no Ash! Don't be silly. Of course you'll have a power. It's just really, really! late. That's all. Why not just say-
"Sorry. I don't... I don't have mine yet..." I answer wearily. or just say that. Well done Ash. She looks down at me for a second. I can't tell if she's silently judging me or not. She then stops typing and hands me a piece of paper.

32

"Oh dear, at 15? That's strange. Well here, you can just choose from these. We have many options here, but the main four are written in bold across the top." she gestures to the top of the paper and I read through them quickly. "Agility? No. elements? No. potions? No. beast-keeping? nope." I whisper to myself as I read. "Illusions? No. bard? No- wait..." I quickly read the extra information underneath the word. Music magic? That could be fun, and easy to fake.

"I think I like the bard magic track. Could I choose that?" I question as I pass back the paper.
"Bold choice, of course you can. But you know without any magical ability it'll be a lot harder for you?" she says, typing on her keyboard once again. I shrug it off. Any of them surely would be more difficult without any actual magic ability. If anything I just sing. See? Easy fix.
"Im sure ill get my power soon, my family actually got theirs late too-"
"Wait? but didn't your family get theirs-" Rose starts to question me but I cut her off with a laugh. The office lady raises an eyebrow but carries on with what she was doing.

"Right, I'm just going to grab you your uniform. I'll be back in a second."

After a few minutes of waiting I was finally given my uniform, and honestly, it's kinda cool. for a uniform anyway. I go into the cubicle and change. It's a branded dark grey short sleeved t-shirt plus white under armour with longer sleeves, as well as black trousers with my black shoes. The black and white is supposed to represent a piano, and everyone's uniform is different. For example, Rose's has the same T-shirt with a skirt but her colours are white and yellow. It's quite smart.
I step out and Rose throws me compliments after compliments, but the teacher doesn't seem to be impressed.

"I'm sorry dear, but we have strict rules on accessories. You can't wear that glove or necklace here." she says with a straight face. She doesn't even look at me.
I look down and hold onto my blue crystal necklace which is now on show. Normally I wear it under my clothes and completely forget about it. I haven't taken it off since…
I hold onto it tightly. For the glove, my scar can easily trigger people, I can just use that as an excuse.

"Woah, I haven't seen that necklace before? Where'd you get it?" Rose pipes up in astonishment.
"Uhm... it was a gift. And, I'm sorry but I can't take them off." I say trying to come across as confident. Tucking my necklace into my T-shirt. "Uh- I have a skin condition that could trigger other people, and for the necklace it's... uh- it's-"
"I see..." she sighs "well for the skin condition, we should have been made aware of that beforehand. And for the necklace, if you insist on wearing it, keep it tucked away today and take it off for tomorrow. Deal?"
"Deal. Thank you Ma'am." I say with a nod. Quickly leaving with Rose.

Ash you gotta be more careful.

6.
Trust in you

Me and Rose start our walk down the corridors and I can't help but feel everyone's eyes on us. Well... on me. But just as I've been taught, I keep my head down and ignore everyone. It's just the best way to go about these things. I need to keep my head down and hide in the back, but when we abruptly come to a stop I'm forced to look up.

"Watch where you're going next time!" I hear someone yell. My eyebrow immediately raises. I turn in the direction of the voice.
"Wait here a moment, ok?" Rose whispers and speed walks over to the cluster of people. I'm baffled. What is she doing? I walk sideways

slightly to get a better view and address the situation.

I see a boy, who can't be much older than 14, on the ground collecting a bunch of books and trying to put them away in his backpack. Before I have a chance to stay anything another girl goes to kick the books out of his hands and everyone just... laughs?

"Excuse me! What is wrong with you all?" I shout, pushing through the cluster of people, which is starting to get bigger, trying to reach the poor boy. I get a few sarcastic comments and quiet mutters in response. They all quickly disperse, everyone including Rose, and now the corridor is almost completely empty. Rose did attempt to come back a few minutes later and help but I told her not to bother. I'll find my own way to class afterwards.

"Are you ok?" I ask as I help him pick up his books.
"I'm- I'm fine.. Thank you..?" he drags, trying to match a name to my face.
"Ash. I'm new. And you are..?" I passed back his books, stood up and offered him my hand, helping him to his feet.
"Max... I'm Max." he responds with a weak smile.

"I'm so sorry Max, they shouldn't be treating you like that." I sigh and cross my arms. I'm still in shock.

"It's fine.. It happens a lot actually. Thank you for helping me."

"Hey, don't worry about it, I couldn't have just stood and watched. I had to do something." I say with a soft smile. He smiles back and then we start walking.

"We should get going, we'll be even later the more we stand out here, and I bet you don't wanna be late to your first lesson on your first day." he laughs. I look up at the clock and curse under my breath.

"Shoot! Uh- and I have no idea where I'm going! Great-"

"It's ok, bard? Right? Me too, I can take you." I look down at him and we start walking.

"ya... but I don't even know what class! And, no offence, but I doubt we're in the same year, let alone the same class."

"None taken! But you're in year 11? Right? I am too!" he laughs when he looks up at my face. How is he-

"You're in year 11? You look- and again, no offence- but you look, like what? 14?" I say in pure astonishment. There is no way we were in the same year. He's almost half the size of me!

"I'm 13, actually. But I'll be 14 soon. I moved up a few years because I wasn't being challenged enough with other kids my age." Woah- this kid must be really good. That's like 2 whole years he jumped! That's pretty impressive. I don't know if a kid could handle the ups and downs of my plan, but he's definitely on my list of possibilities.
"That's pretty cool dude. Well done." he looks down at the ground with a sad smile, he doesn't reply straight away.

"Thank you Ash…"

In no time we made it to our classroom. I see the teacher talking to the students and my hands go to reach for my necklace. Out of habit. It's my first day and I'm late, that really isn't the first impression I was hoping to give. Max must notice my discomfort because he starts comforting me.

"Hey, don't worry! Our teacher really isn't so bad. Trust me. You'll be fine." Before I can thank him he pushes the door wide open and walks in calmly. God, I wish I had the confidence to do that. But I don't. So I just awkwardly stood in the doorway, feeling all the students' eyes on me.

"Morning, Max. you are a little later than i'd have liked you to be dear." she says, but although she's folding her arms she doesn't seem upset, or angry. The calmness in her voice shocks me.
If I was ever late before- I was bound to get a huge ear full before being shut away for the rest of the day. But... no. Ash. remember. You're not there anymore. You know how they treated you was wrong, you don't have to deal with that anymore! You aren't stuck there anymore. You're free now. you're back in the real world and you won't be-

"Oh, who is this? Max? Did you make a new friend?" The teacher's voice made me jump, I guess I was getting a little too lost in my head. I take another step into the classroom and hold my hands behind me back, maybe that way they won't see them shaking.
"Oh yeah. I'm... It's my first day. I'm Ash. Ash spring..." I can immediately hear all the whispers when I say my last name. The teacher looks slightly shook for a moment, then goes over to her computer, starts typing, then scrolls and stands back up.
"Ah yes, your name has just been added to my register. I'll be your teacher for this year, Ash.

feel free to sit in any empty seat." I awkwardly thanked her and sheepishly made my way to the back of the classroom where Max was seated. He was sitting beside a window with a complete empty row beside him. I drop down my backpack and pull out the chair closest to his. Feeling everyone's eyes still on me, I sink deep into the chair, trying my hardest to disappear.

"Hey, it's ok. You did great." he says in a soft whisper. "Our teacher is definitely one of the nicest here, she won't hold one late mark against you at all. And, I mean, the class isn't that bad either. Just don't cross them at break." I try to laugh with him but it doesn't come out the way I wanted it to. I scan the room again, most people have seen my talking with Max and are now pointing and whispering, looking either disgusted or unbothered. I start to wonder why these guys don't like him. I know I've only known him for a brief minute but he honestly doesn't seem that bad. I mean- it could easily be because of jealousy, you know, the year 9 moves up 2 years and shows all the actual year 11s up.
I know I'd probably be slightly intimidated if something happened like that in one of my classes back- wait...

The lesson ended fairly quickly and Max was right, it's quite hard to dislike or be scared of our teacher, who I learned a little later on was called Miss J. Also, Max is really sweet, I don't necessarily want to call him a 'friend' yet but, one day. Maybe.
He could easily be my friend and be the first on my team. As long as he is relatively calm under larger amounts of pressure then he is a good fit

7.
Half of you

At lunch I choose to sit down on the spare table at the back. I think I'd rather stay out of the way, people watching is way more fun than actually socialising anyway. I was originally going to sit with Rose, but after this morning, I'd rather not. I'm still shocked about how quickly she turned. She turned into a completely different person. Oh, and I'm not sure if I'm at the part with Max where we sit next to each other during our free time just yet. So I'm now just sitting in the corner, with my book and sandwich waiting for the bell.
But just as I'm about to dive into another world, I hear a voice behind me.

"Hey! Ash! Why are you sitting all alone?" Max asks, quickly taking the seat beside me. I run my hand through my hair, laughing awkwardly.

Then I notice someone, who I haven't seen before, sitting opposite us.

"Oh yeah, and this is my twin, Bleu!" I don't even get to say 'hi' because they quickly reach over the table and shake my hand.

"Hey! I'm Bleu, they/them. Max has told me a lot about you at break! Oh and I love your hair! And this glove! It's so cool. How did you get away with wearing it? Oh my gosh, by the way-"

"Bleu, calm down a little. Give them a bit more space." Max says with a laugh. I laugh too. Bleu quickly apologies and sits back down.

"Haha, it's ok. It's nice to meet you Bleu, I'm Ash-" I go to continue my introduction but stop to think. Just to check what I'm about to say feels right. "Uh- they/them. Too." I finally say. They suddenly jump up and I look over at Max, slightly confused.

"Oh my gosh! I left my water bottle in my locker! I'll be right back!" and with that they disappear. I chuckle along with Max.

"I'm sorry about them, they're always so hyper."

"It's ok, don't worry, they kind of remind me of my brother-" Max's head immediately turns to face me. shoot-

"You have a brother? wait- of course you do. Almost everyone knows that. Is he at this

school now too?" I swallow hard at his question. My smile falters as I look down at my sandwich, thinking up an excuse.
"Uh- he's- he's uh- travelling. Yeah. he's away travelling." somehow that didn't seem believable. Maybe it's because I know I'm lying. I know it's not true, but I've lied plenty of times before, I'm almost a certified liar. Why was this so difficult to say?
And, I mean, it's not like he's not ok. He's as safe as he can be. But I just hate thinking of his reaction the morning after I left. I'm fed up with seeing his face everywhere, carrying the most disappointed and hurt expression ever.
my body starts to burn up. I feel sick. I excuse myself so I can grab a glass of water and go to stand in front of the table that the water is on, unsure on what to do.
I put my hands on the edge of the table and hang my head, feeling slightly dizzy. Why? Why do I put myself in these situations?

"Ash? Are you ok?" I hear Max whisper through the ragging noise in the background. I take a few deep breaths and turn around, smiling, as if nothing happened.
"Yeah. I'm fine." I say as I approach the table and take my seat. Acting completely oblivious.

"Ok…" He says slowly. We drop the topic and Max goes to start eating his lunch while I pick up my book. But once again, just before I can get into it, he calls for my attention.

"Uh- Ash?" I snap my head around, a little too aggressively, as he points to the end of our table, which is only two seats away.
"What is it-?" As I question, I notice a certain brown haired girl looking really out of place. She shifts to the side and holds her lunch tray out in front of her. I drop my book, cross my arms and look away, shutting her out. I immediately feel more defensive, as if my walls have just rebuilt themselves.
"Please.. Ash.. can I sit with you? I really want to talk to-"
"No. You don't need to talk to me about anything. And you won't." I say, turning around slowly.
"Are- are we cool?" The question makes me laugh.
"like ice. Now please leave us alone." I make it obvious I'm faking a smile which she doesn't appreciate. She rolls her eyes and sighs.
"Please Ash. you haven't even heard me out. You can't cut someone out without listening to them first." I don't even need to think of my reply.

46

"I can't. But I am. You left me to help others bully a kid! For what? I don't see how you could possibly explain your way outta that one." I spit out. When I look at her I can see she has her pre-built walls up, but I can almost see through a small crack in them.
"Look. I'm sorry. I know they are bad people, they do bad things. But I- It's... I can't stop them. I don't know how to. And I never actually did anything! Please- I promise I'll start standing up to them- I just- don't know how to yet." I can hear in her voice that what she's saying is genuine, but I'm still annoyed, so I stood up and walked next to her. My boiling blood blistering my skin.

"Rose. Sure, you didn't physically do anything. But by laughing along with the mass amount of other people who were also 'just laughing' you created a worse state in his head. Just by laughing you made it seem like his misery was entertainment for you all. Maybe you don't know this because, to me, you seem like the person who has always been in these sorta cliques, but having a large group of people bigger, stronger and mentally louder than you is worse than having someone physically pushing you around like a dog with a chew toy. Maybe you don't know that because you've

never been bullied before but trust me, it's true." I didn't realise that while talking, a few loose tears started to spill, I wiped them away and stood my ground. I've got about half the hall's eyes on me now but I don't care.
Rose is looking up at me, completely baffled. Stunned almost. She doesn't seem like she has anything to say so I finalise the conversation.
"Since you have nothing left to say, you should be on your way. Hm?" I say simply, walking away and taking my seat. She just continues to stand there. Dumbfounded.
"Off you go." I repeat. Picking up my book and ignoring her presence.
As if on cue I hear a voice a little way away call out to Rose to get away from 'those freaks' which just makes me laugh.
"I… I'm sorry." was what she said as she walked away. Sure, she still does sound genuine, and there's a high chance I bruised her ego, but I don't feel bad about what I said. It needed to be said. And I'm glad the rest of the hall heard me. Maybe everyone will think twice about bullying anyone else from now on.

A little after Rose walked off, Bleu approached our table. Looking shocked and… worried?

"Was that Rose? Why was she here? What did she say? Did she do anything?" they ask frantically. I sigh, knock down my walls, and reassure them.
"She didn't have the chance. Ash put her in her place!" Max says proudly. Tapping me on the back afterwards. I just brush it off. Anyone could have done that, it just happened to be me.
"Yeah I heard from the hall! That was really brave, Ash. well done." I try to thank them but it doesn't feel right. I mean, I just stood up for a friend to a friend, I didn't do anything particularly special.
"Why would Rose wanna know if you two were cool? Though? Like- were you friends or something?" Max hesitates. I put down my book and sigh again.
 "I live with her family." As I say this, in the most simple way this could have been said, Bleu and Max both, at the same time, spit out their drinks in shock. I raise an eyebrow.
"You- wait. you know Rose? Like Rose paramore Rose? And not only that but- you live with her?" Bleu asks. Wiping the water off the table as they do.
"Yeah. Her older sister is like my best friend. And Rose isn't that bad. She's normally really sweet, and quiet. That's probably why what she

did this morning shocked me. But I'm sure she won't do it again."

"But wait- why would you shout at her like that if you were friends? I'd never be able to be like that with my friends." Max chips in, seeming genuinely interested.

"Because, if I was acting like a complete idiot, I'd like someone to tell me. And I tend to find, if things come from people closer to you, it means more. It sticks more. Because if a stranger said something to you, it would mean nothing, because they're a stranger, someone you'll probably only speak to once. But to hear something like that from someone close to you, it tends to hit deeper because there's no sugar coating, or silver lining. It's completely raw and true, and you're telling them because you care about them and want them to be their best self. I'll get back to hers later and we'll, hopefully, be fine. Because I opened and closed a wound no one else was willing to do for her." Max and Bleu both just looked at me for a minute, then at each other, probably just taking in what I said.

"I- I actually understand that." Max then says. I nod and start packing up my stuff, the bell will go any second now, there's no point in me trying to eat or read now.

"Yeah. I understand as well... You know, Ash, you're a really good friend." The words freeze me in place. 'A good friend'... I shake it off and point out that we should probably start heading to our lessons. The twins agree and we make our way through the bustling corridors in silence.

8.
Everyone but you

Honestly, I thought this school would be worse, but then again, it's not hard to be better than the school I grew up in, and ever since my little speech, about 2 weeks ago, Not a single person has been bullied. Well, I haven't personally seen anyone being wronged anyway. The only downside is I've not found anyone else capable of joining my resistance yet. I've been planning attack strategies and timings non stop, but all of it is useless without accomplices.

The bell has just gone for lunch and me and Rose are making our way to the hall, but as we are walking someone appears in front of us, making Rose abruptly stop in her tracks. She hugs her books into her chest and moves a loose hair strand that falls from her ponytail behind her ear.

"Hey Rose!" the girl says in a sweet tone. Also carrying books against her chest.

"Hey... Val," she stammers, scanning the corridor, as if looking for an exit. "Uh- how are you?" she adds after a small pause. Val clearly doesn't notice the awkward tension between them by the way she smiles.

"I'm good, how are you?" Rose doesn't respond, she looks like she's completely forgotten to speak. Now I'm starting to feel the tension. I roll my eyes and hold out my hand.

"Hi, I'm Rose's friend. Ash." I introduce myself and Val's attention moves onto me. Rose can thank me for that later.

"Oh! Your Ash. I heard about what happened at lunch on your first day. Honestly, I applaud you, and it seems you've both patched that gap up." I nod with a soft laugh. "I'm Valerie, Val for short." She shakes my hand and I glance over at Rose, who has completely shut down, but then I notice the sudden change of pigment in her cheeks. Ohhh! Ok ok. I think I understand the situation now.

"Well, i've gotta get going now, I'll be late to return these to the library otherwise. Well it was nice meeting you Ash, and nice seeing you too Rose, we really need to catch up some

53

time! Anyway, see ya!" she then practically skips off down the hall and into the library. As soon as she's out of sight I start laughing hysterically!

"It's not funny!"
"Yes. Yes, it is funny! Little Rose is so in love!" I tease playfully as we continue our walk.
"Ugh fine! Sure, ok. Maybe I have a little crush! Now will you stop!" she sighs, stopping at the door to the hall. I try to contain my laughter and put my hands up in defence.
"Alright alright. I'll stop." I promise, smirking playfully.
"Even after 7 years, you're still as annoying as ever." I pretend to act hurt and hold back another laughing fit. She rolls her eyes and playfully nudges my side before walking into the hall. I wait a little while and then enter, heading straight towards Max and Bleu. Max has his back to me but Bleu notices me instantly, they wave wildly and ushers me to the seat beside them.

"Hey guys, how are you both?" I ask as I take my seat.
"I'm good, just tired. I uh- I've been studying all night." Max responds with a sigh, I pat him on the back sympathetically and look at Bleu.

"I'm pretty good! I actually found this new TV show last night and watched it till way past 3 this morning! it 's amazing! Definitely a new favourite of mine! Oh and me and Max-"
"Hey Bleu? Maybe Ash doesn't want to hear about every little thing we did last night." he says with a weak smile. I can tell Bleu is slightly hurt but forces a smile when he nods.
"No no, it's ok. I don't mind. Honestly." I say in reassurance, making Bleu seem slightly happier, but they still don't continue with what they were saying.
"I'm sorry Bleu, but you know it's not a good idea, you know, going around and sharing absolutely everything." Max says apologetically. I smile simply between the two as they mutually agree on something.
Whatever it was, it felt too personal for me to ask questions on.
I reach into my backpack for my book but just as I'm about to, the bell rings, signally the end of lunch.
"Already! Seriously- I swear lunch is getting quicker and quicker with each passing day!" I joke, causing the other two to laugh. I pack up my things and stand up.
"They must be slowly making lessons longer each day, and they'll keep doing it until we have no free time left." Bleu groans. Me and

Max looked at each other, then I turned back to them.
"Maybe. Who knows?" I shrug, laughing as I walk off. I can hear Max laughing with me as Bleu starts to get worried.
"Wait? Really!" I hear them shout out from behind.

The bell eventually rings to indicate the end of the school day. I skip out of my class, saying goodbye to Max, then to Bleu and catch up to Rose just outside the back gates. We start our walk and I spot a familiar brown haired girl across from us, standing in line at a local ice cream van. I quickly turn to Rose, who is completely oblivious.

"Look! Rose! There's an ice cream van! We have to grab something." I say excitedly, pulling on her arm, trying to divert her over to the truck.
"But I don't have any money- woah-"
I drag her across the street despite her protest and stand in line, whipping out my purse from my trouser pocket, pulling out a £10 note from inside. I think I can spare a bit of cash on this.
"How-? alright. fine. But then we go straight home." I nod and wait patiently in line. Clearly

she still hasn't spotted Val yet so I've gotta tug some more strings here.
"Oh hey! Isn't that that girl from lunch?" I shout out a little too loud, pretending to just notice her. She spins around on her heel and waves at us both. Rose spins around herself and immediately tenses up. It's hard not to laugh.
"Hey! How are you both?" she asks as she approaches us. I smile sheepishly in Rose's direction as a simple 'your welcome'. Maybe she doesn't see the point in thanking me yet, but she will.
"I'm great! Uhm I'm just about to order our ice creams. What did you want? My treat." I offer, she tries to refuse, saying she's happy to pay for herself, but I insist, and win.
"You two should talk, I won't be long."

I quickly reach the front of the que and repeat our order, listening in on their conversation behind me. Though, it's not really a conversation, Rose really hasn't said an actual word at all.
"Gracias." I thank, passing over my money and telling the young woman manning the truck to keep the change. She told me to have a nice day then I walked up to Rose and Val, passing over their order and acting as if I didn't just push Rose into her worst nightmare. They'd

taken a seat at a nearby bench, so I sat on the arm beside Val and jumped into their very one-sided conversation. Then I noticed the bench is similar to the one in that picture back at the paramore's home, but I don't let that get to me. This isn't about me.

"Uhm, Val? Right? The one from the corridor?" I ask, passing over the cones.
"Yep, that's me, and thanks again for the ice cream. I still don't mind paying you back for it. I know money isn't easy to get a hold of."
"Don't be silly, If that's true, I don't want you wasting yours on snacks," I joke, "Trust me, it's no biggie." She laughs and thanks me again. Then I look over at Rose who has, once again, fallen silent and turned a deep red. I've seen and read enough romance shows and novels to be able to tell she's clearly flustered.
"So, Val, we're actually planning a little meet up for pizza and bowling on Saturday,"
"Oh really?" she says, looking between me and Rose.
"Yeah, really?" I hear Rose mutter something else but I ignore it.
"Yeah, and we were wondering if you wanted to join us?" I asked cooly. Someone had to do it.

"Oh- uh, I'd love to!" I take her phone number and notice Rose watching us in bewilderment. I then wave goodbye as she leaves and sit beside Rose with a smug expression on my face.

"I hate you dude." she says, shaking her head.
"What? Why?" I ask, trying to act offended, but I just laugh instead. "Everyone else can clearly see that something is obviously going on between you too. Someone had to say something to start rolling that ball, so I did." I state obviously.
"Well now you need to find other people who are free Saturday, there is no way we can only go as a trio." She seems to think I'm jumping into this idea completely blind, as if I didn't think of a solution to every tiny issue while ordering our food. But, spoiler alert, I did.

"Easy. Leila, Max and Bleu. there. Now there's 6."
"Ok but-"
"I'm already looking for a place to go. I was thinking of going to that shopping centre, you know, the big one in the city centre with the swimming pool, bowling alley, cinema and restaurants all on the top floor?" I announce, pulling out my phone and searching it up.

"Did you really think of an answer to every question in the short amount of time you were over there?" she asks.
"Yep!" I say triumphantly.
"I still hate you. But I will admit. You really know how to quickly plan something on the spot." she laughs. I laugh too, but not for as long.
"Yo también te amo amiga" And then we continue our walk home.

9.
Magic hands

Saturday rolls around pretty fast. I'm just buttoning up my jacket in front of Leila's mirror when Rose comes barging in.

"Ash? There you are! Are you ready? We're gonna be late!" I spin around and see her nervously standing in the doorway, and honestly, I'm a little taken aback. She looks really good.
She's wearing a white top with short sleeves that have small sewn on flowers around the cuffs, a maroon coloured skirt that stops just above her knee with plain black leggings and socks, plus red and white high tops. To top it all off she has silver dangling earrings and a dark red clutch purse. I start fidgeting with my

own silver sun and moon earrings, which I completely forgot I was wearing.
"Woah girl? Who are you trying to impress?" Leila cuts in before I have a chance to speak. I haven't told her about the true intentions behind this afternoon, but by the way she's smiling at her baby sister, she can clearly tell something is up.
"What? no one!" she exclaims defensively. Her cheeks are quick to betray her.
"Ok." she sings in response. I can't help but laugh. I quickly put on my shoes and grab my bag from the back of Leila's desk chair.
"We're just meeting our friends." I remind her, trying to help Rose out. I'm not about to expose her love life to her older sister, that's a bit far.
"Alright, Well, have fun you two. And bring me back one of those pretzels please!" Leila unfortunately couldn't come with us because she already made plans but I promised to fill her in once I got back.
"Will do! Adios!" I wave as we exit the room. Mrs Paramore is waiting impatiently outside the house when we leave.
"God, you kids took your time. Come on!" I smile and apologise to her as she holds open the car door but I notice Rose rolling her eyes. I don't think too much of it and we start our short journey to the city centre.

"Ash? Is that really all you could pull together?" Rose asks me when we reach the shopping centre, looking me up and down. I scan over my own outfit.
I'm wearing baggy light blue jeans along with my usual white short sleeve t-shirt, a black varsity jacket with brown sleeves finished with blue trainers and a red tote bag.
"Yes, because we are just bowling and eating out with a few friends. Anyway, I thought this was quite smart." I adjust my tote bag on my shoulder as we step onto the escalator.
"Baggy clothes aren't smart Ash." she states, I let out a quick chuckle.
"Either way, I'm dressed casually, you're the one looking as if you're trying to impress someone. Oh wait, you are." I say, playfully nudging her. She rolls her eyes and walks off the escalator a little ahead of me.
"Watch it." She attempts to threaten me. I burst into laughter.
We reached the top floor and are now standing, waiting for the others to show. I look over to Rose and notice her hair tied up in that same high ponytail, but some strands are starting to fall out.

"Hey? Rose?"

"Yeah?"
"Maybe you should leave your hair down, it looks better." I say, carefully pulling her hair band out. I adjust her hair slightly by brushing it with my pocket brush and try to style it better. She automatically looks way better. I really don't know why she keeps it up so much anyway, her subtle brown and pink waves are really pretty.
"There you go." I announce, passing her the mirror. She looks into it for a minute, unsure of what to think.
"Thank you…" I smile and take back my mirror.

"So? What have you planned for today then?" I reach into my bag for my phone as she asks.
"So I've booked us 2 games of bowling for 12 0'clock and they will take about an hour each, roughly, so that'll bring us to 2. I've then booked a table at the Pizza Hut for 3, so we have about one extra hour to look around the shops or to play in the arcades, and what we didn't get to do before we can just do after food." I say, scrolling through my notes app.
"Woah! You've really thought this through huh?"
"Yep!" I agree proudly.
I like to be prepared and organised for… Well, anything! It avoids those awkward moments

where everyones sits around unsure of what to do or say. Having a plan is always a good way to secure success.

"Hey Ash!" I hear a familiar voice say from behind me. Smiling, I spin around on my heel. Seeing Max and Bleu approaching us in jeans and matching sweaters. I wave them over.
"Hey guys!" I walk over to them and give them a high five, then take them over to Rose and introduce them, thinking she probably doesn't really know them that well.
"Rose, this is Bleu and this is their twin Max-!"
"Wait? Max? I thought-" My eyebrow immediately raises as Max cuts her off.
"No. nope. Max. it's Max." he says with a nervous laugh. I take time to study the clear tension rising between them both.
"Ok..?" I say slowly. That was weird.
Everyone starts shifting awkwardly in their places and I can only guess that something was about to come out that Max didn't want to be said around me.
Pft! For a second I thought I was gonna have to edit my recruit list, thinking that that something may jeopardise Max's ability in battle, but that's stupid.
Wait-

"So, you said there were 5 of us playing? Who's the fifth?" Bleu asks excitedly, breaking through the tension and my train of thought. I shake off my worries and smile.
"Oh yeah! I actually invited-" And just as I'm about to say Val Rose punches my arm and points towards the steps. "Ow! That hurt- oh! Val! Hey!" Rose starts waving with a shaky smile while I point her out to the twins.
"Hey Rose! Hey Ash!" She greets with a wide smile. "Thanks again for inviting me!"
"It's no problem!" I brush off. She turns to Max and Bleu.
"Hey! I'm Val. nice to meet you." she shakes their hands as they introduce themselves. I can't help but smile.

I'm happy to see them getting along. At least I know that if I were to recruit Val, she's good with other people. That's a good trait to have, and a necessary one.

After everyones got to know each other a little more we made our way to the bowling alley. I confirm our spot, grab our shoes, find our lane and start our first game.
I don't actually think I've been bowling before. Well.. definitely not since-

"Ash! It's your turn!" bleu shouts over the background noise. I walk over to the tray of bowling balls and smile, testing a few different weights.

I start swinging the ball, focusing on the arrows on the lane then letting the ball roll to the centre one. I jump as the ball hits the pins, noticing after that I knocked all the 10 pins down.

"Woah! Great shot!" Rose shouts, patting me on the back. I back away, taking a seat with a chuckle.

"Beginners luck?" I laugh, causing bleu to spin around and jump over to me.

"This is your first time! Oh my god! How did you get a strike when you've never played before? That's awesome!" They say, completely astonished.

"Well it's all about where you aim for the ball to go. You can't aim too far ahead, you won't guarantee it will reach that spot. So you aim for somewhere closer, the arrows on the floor are a good place. That way, when it rolls over that middle arrow, there's a much higher chance it'll hit the middle pin. Oh and, making sure you're more or less rolling it on the ground rather than throwing it, it helps with accuracy." I start to explain in a 'duh' tone. You don't have to be a genius to know that. Yet all 4 of them are now looking at me as if I just solved world hunger. "I have been playing this game for as long as I can remember. How come I never knew that!" Val complains. They all start to agree with her and then it starts to settle in. I swallow hard.

Needless to say we all got a lot of strikes after that. When we asked for a copy of the scoreboard afterwards the lady at the desk was pretty impressed with us. And I did in fact win both rounds. I myself am shocked I won, a good aim was something I always lacked. Apparently...

Everyone was smiling and laughing when we left and we still had just over an hour till our table was ready. I suggest going into the big arcade a few doors down. We skip towards it and immediately start changing our notes for coins. I don't change as much as everyone else, so I ended up just standing and watching the others play. They all look so happy, even Rose, who has stopped stuttering and is now having full on conversations with Val. They are now playing together on the dance machine while Max and Bleu are racing each other in Mario kart, but after their last round ends Bleu runs off to try to win a teddy bear with a pink and blue ribbon and Max is playing on the 2p machines beside them.

They all just seem so... genuine.

"They all seem so happy. Don't they?" Max says, suddenly appearing at my side, speaking my mind. I jump, then nod.
"Why are you just standing here? Go join in!" he then adds, tugging lightly on my arm. I don't move.

"Sometimes... I prefer to stop and... just observe, I guess. Taking in everything and everyone else around me." I say with a sigh. I thought I'd replied quiet enough that he couldn't hear me, but somehow he did
"Yeah. I guess I know what you mean." he says, leaning against the machine behind us.
I lean back as well. We both don't say anything until I realise that this might be a good time to ask him about that awkward moment when he got here. I have to know, It's been bugging me. I'm not the best at forgetting stuff like that, I've always been a curious person.
"Max? Why was Rose so confused earlier? When I introduced you, what was she about to say that you didn't want her too?" As I ask, he stiffens up.

"Oh. uh… I… uh-" he stammers while playing with his nails.
"Don't worry, I won't tell anyone, not if you don't want me to." I say, hoping it'll comfort him enough so he feels like he can tell me. I mean, I'm only interested because, if it affects my plans, I need to know. And if it's not, it's completely irrelevant and not of any use to me, so I have no need to tell anyone else if that's what he's worried about.

"My birth name… uhm- it's not actually Max-" He says finally, looking down at the colourful yet probably very dirty carpet.
"Oh.." Is that it?
"Is it a nickname? Sorry, for being nosy." I ask, unsure of what to say.
"Uhm no… it's- uh- I'm… I'm trans…" he shuts his eyes tight when he says that. Wait? He's what? I immediately soften up a little.
"Oh… Thanks for telling me…" I'm honestly not 100% sure what to say in this type of situation. So I put a hand on his shoulder and said the first thing I could think of. "You're really brave, Max, and I won't tell anyone if you don't want me to." he lifts up his head to look at me properly, that's when I notice that he'd been silently crying.

"You're... you're a really good friend. I'm so glad I met you..." as he blinks a few loose tears force their way down his cheeks. I pull him into a hug and let him cry into my jacket.

A friend...?

10.
Are you..?

After we finished our games we all happily made our way to the restaurants on the other side of the floor. We all ordered our food, gossiping and laughing over the duration of our meal, I mean, they were, I was sort of just... listening. I mean, I answered one or two questions thrown in my direction, but for the most part, I didn't really say anything. The others fill up on pizza and unlimited salad and decide it's probably time to start heading back. I take the bill, collect everyone's change and pay the rest myself, not that they know that though. We exit the restaurant saying our goodbyes while Rose calls her mum.

"Thanks Ash! This has been the best afternoon!" Bleu says excitedly. I match their energy and smile.
"It has! We should definitely do it again sometime! Bye guys!"

Rose is now off the phone and is saying her goodbyes to Val. I wait till she leaves to approach her, giving them both some space.
"So my mums not able to drive us back." her tone of voice changes instantly. I hear a frustrated sigh escape her lips and we start walking out. "She's still with her stupid work friends so now we gotta walk home." she then tenses up, I notice and play a smile.
"That's ok! I'm sure it won't take us too long to get back."

The beginning of our walk was pretty quiet, so I tried multiple different ways of sparking conversation, mainly because the silence was making me feel strange.

"So... you and Val seem to be getting closer," I point out, hoping for some sort of acknowledgement.
"Yeah, I guess." she doesn't even look up from her phone.
"Hey? What's wrong? You don't seem like yourself." I quiz, giving her a puzzled look.
"Nothing. I'm fine. It's just-" Just as she's about to tell me what's wrong we both stop as something small and dark runs in front of us and under a cafe sign. Rose squeals and jumps back, but I don't.

Of course, something had to steal our attention just as I'm about to get an answer.

"Ah! What in the world was that?" she screams. The fact that she's actually scared makes me laugh.
"Probably just a rat or something." I replied calmly, freaking her out more. I kneel down and look under the sign, just to check whatever it was was ok.
"What! Hey! Ash, don't go near it!" I tried to reassure her that it was fine but she didn't listen. So I focus on the small creature cowering under this sign.
I move the sign to the side and see a small black kitten, rather than a rat.
"Awh!" I squeal, as I reach and pick it up.
"It's just a little kitten." I clarify quickly, mainly so Rose doesn't start running off down the street. I picked it up and showed it to her.
"Ok ok.. That's not too bad."She puts her hand on her chest as she takes a few deep breaths. "But I'm pretty sure you shouldn't just pick up a stray cat, and a black cat at that." I stop cuddling up to the little baby and raise an eyebrow at her. "You know. Black cats are deemed unlucky, and strays are normally dirty and full of diseases." I ignore her stereotypes and continue gushing over the kitten.

"But look how cute it is! And I couldn't care less about some silly myth that probably isn't even true. I think all cats are beautiful!" She clearly disagrees with me but doesn't say anything. I hold the cat out in front of me and immediately feel some sort of connection with it. Though, I'm not sure why.
"Your mum wouldn't mind if I brought it back to the house, right?" I hope so.
"What! You wanna bring it home?"
"Yeah! Look at its little face! You can't tell me it's not adorable. Don't worry if the cost to take care of it is the problem, I'm pretty sure I'll be able to afford it." Rose looks around awkwardly, she seems worried. But I ignore it and play my puppy eye's card, hoping to convince her.
"Uh- uhm.. Ugh fine!" she eventually gives in and I jump for joy as if I was a little kid. I cuddle the little thing close and then we continue our walk.
"Hear that little guy? I'll take care of you!" I act as if it can hear me, but I know it can't. Obviously.
I've never heard of someone actually being able to talk to animals. well, not someone without a magical ability that allows them to do so, anyway. But even then, the animal doesn't talk to you, they just understand you.

The whole way back I coo over my new kitten, but Rose goes back to not speaking, though this time, she seems to be more stressed? Rather than annoyed.

"Here we are, little guy! Your new home!" I say proudly as we approach the Paramore's house. I then get a sudden sense to act cautiously but I'm not sure why. So I, once again, ignored the feeling until it disappeared.
"Right Ash… uh- take it straight upstairs. Please?" I turn to face her as I open the door.
"It's fine Rose. you don't need too-"
"Ahem. Girls?" As I spin around to walk inside I see Mrs Paramore standing in the doorway. Her arms crossed and her eyebrows furrowed. Calmly, I hold up my spare hand and wave as I enter.
"Hey, Mrs Paramore. How was your afternoon/evening?" As I speak with confidence Rose trembles beside me, almost caving under her mothers shade.
"Good, thank you. Now head upstairs, dear." I nod and take my new kitten and Rose towards the stairs, but Rose gets stopped.
"Not you." was all Mrs Paramore said. I look across my shoulder and see a scared expression plastered on her face.

76

"It's ok. I'll wait up on the landing for you." as Mrs Paramore pulls Rose out of the hall, I begin to suspect something slightly off, but assume it's nothing important. I shrug it off and make my way upstairs. As I reach the first landing Leila suddenly appears in front of me.
"Woah! You scared me bro." I laugh, punching her arm jokingly. But... she doesn't laugh? Why didn't she-

"Where's Rose?" She asks while trying to get past me. I raise an eyebrow.
"Uh- your mum took her over there, I'm assuming to the living room. Why?"
"Damn it. Rose!" Leila dashes down the staircase and straight into the living room. I'm left completely baffled.
"What in the world is-?"

Then I heard it...

"Don't touch her!" It's muffled but clear as day.

Out of instinct I drop everything and run. I run up to my room and slam the door. My breathing starts to speed up and my palms start sweating. I run to the furthest corner and curl up. I try to calm myself down but it's no use. I rest my head on my knees as my body shakes uncontrollably. For a moment, I feel as if my soul has left entirely.

***

"Don't touch her!" he screams as he stands between me and Miss Wicker, taking my hit for me. I continue to cry.
"Keep a better watch of your sister. Cadete." She instructs cooly, storming out of the room. I drop down to the floor in a puddle of my own tears.
"hey...Ashley. It's ok. You're ok now... I've got you.." he places his hands on my shoulders and I close my eyes.
"Calm down... Ashley. Ashley?"

***

"Ash? Ash! Wake up! Ash!" as soon as the voice changes my smile falters. I do, however, start forcing myself awake. When I finally come too, I notice Leila hovering over me. From the feeling of carpet under my hands, I'm assuming I'm on my bedroom floor.
"Oh my goodness! I thought I had lost you! Again!" she moves so she's crouched beside me. I jolt up right and my breathing goes unsteady again.

78

"Wait! Where's... where is-?"
"Where is who? Rose?" she pulls her hands away from me.
"No... uh-" I struggle to answer as I try to catch my breath. Feeling really dizzy from my sudden jolt. I put a hand to my chest and closed my eyes again.
"Ash calm down, You'll pass out again." she tries to help me over to my bed while I continue to stutter. We sit on the edge of the mattress and she holds me up right.
"A- A... Alex! he s- he helped me!" I finally cried.
"Alex? Wait- as in your brother?" I nod my head violently.
"I thought... I thought he was dead?" my head snaps in her direction, my vision blurry.
"N- no. I-"
"Ash. calm down. Did you hit your head? I'll grab you some water. yeah?" Her smile is soft and somehow helps to steady my breathing a little. I nod and wipe my eyes.

He's not dead... he's trapped.

"Here's your water.." Leila passes over a small glass of water a few minutes later. I nurse it in my palms and watch the ripples as I swish it around. Then I take a single sip.

"Are you feeling better now? You really had me freaked…" I sigh and she pulls me into a side hug.
"A little better. Thank you." She sits with me in silence for a little bit, then stands up.
"Right, I've gotta go see Rose. Are you sure you're ok?" She looks right into my eyes, places a gentle hand on my shoulder and waits for me to answer. I nod and take another sip of water. She smiles softly and makes her way out my room and down the stairs to Rose's room.
I stare ahead at the wall blankly, unsure of what exactly I should be thinking of or doing. Everything only starts to hit me when a small black kitten jumps and curls up in my lap. Now a strange new feeling is brewing in my chest, and I don't like it.

"That's why she was so nervous. It makes sense now." I mutter to myself. I briefly think about what happened to Rose because of one of my decisions but I quickly get distracted by the angel in my lap.
"So? What should I name you?" I say as if I was expecting a reply. But I obviously won't get one.
"How about… Misty? You're giving me Misty vibes. Do you like that name?" I stroke her as I

speak. Honestly, something was almost screaming that name to me. But that's probably normal. Right? That's how parents choose names for their children isn't it? Through gut feeling?

11.
Gotta get moving

"Ash? Come here for a second!" Leila shouts. I assume, by the volume and direction of her voice, that she's down on the middle floor. probably at the bottom of the staircase. I put down my pen, notebook and headed down to her.

"What's up?"
"Have you seen the recent rumours?" I give her a confused look, indicating that I haven't.
"There are rumours going around about how Ventura may have outsiders living in plain sight" she says in the type of voice you'd use to tell a scary story around a campfire. My eyes immediately widened. I swallow hard and laugh awkwardly.
"Where would people get that idea from?" I'm trying to make it seem like my hands are shaking right now, I'm not sure if it's working though.

"Honestly, I'm not too sure, I just heard about it through one of my friends, thought you probably would wanna know too." She pulls out her phone and starts scrolling through her messages, then passes it over and shows me the conversation between her and this girl. I read through it and feel slightly sick.

How have people got a hold of this?

"Yeah, apparently there were three campers or something, they came back with loads of stories. I don't know. Like I said it's all just rumours anyway and I doubt it's anything to worry about. Ventura is known to be one of the safest places after all."
yes. Ventura is said to be a harmonious and safe island, one of the safest places in the world. My family has kept a hold of that peace for centuries.

But I know the truth…

"Well uh… thanks for telling me. But I've got quite a lot of homework to do, oh, and I've gotta feed Misty." I say, in a rush to return to my room.

83

"Ok. Wait... who's Misty?" I hear her ask, but I'm already halfway up the stairs. There's really no time for an introduction right now.
"Uh- my cat. Gotta go!" I shout down to her just before I slam my door, breathing heavily.
I rummage around for my phone and check the date.

How dare I not keep a better track of the day! How could I be so stupid? This is what happens when you let your guard down. I'm running dangerously low on time. I've not even got an official plan, let alone a decent team. Nothing is nowhere near the level I require it to be.

"Monday 26th of september..." I whisper to myself, disbelief flowing through every syllable. Suddenly I start to feel dizzy again.
grasping my head, I take a seat at my desk. I'm assuming if I wait a little while It'll settle down, but it doesn't. I rest my head on my desk and close my eyes.

***

"Come on! Ashley, we need to get to the hall!" Alex rushes me. I tie up my long, wavy hair and run out the bathroom door.

"I'm sorry! My hair really isn't my friend today." I groan, adjusting the potions of my ponytail slightly. He chuckles and we start leaving.

"So? What do you think this meeting is about?" I ask curiously. I think it's going to be about a rule Miss Wicker wants to issue. Since that's all it ever is. She's always trying to find new ways to control us.
"I'm hoping for information about our 'big mission'. We've been here for years! Yet they haven't told us anything!" I just laugh.
"Yeah right. Anyway, I bet I can get to the meeting hall before you!" while I speak my speed increases slowly, obviously so I can get a head start, but he runs straight past me.
"Nu-uh!" he shouts, suddenly flying down the corridor. I smile as I sprint over to him, then I remember that I made shortcuts for these situations. I wait for him to turn the first corner and sneakily run through the door leading outside. When outside I clamber and run around the many big metal blocks until I find the one containing the meeting hall. I jump down and enter through the secret door I found while playing hide and seek when I was younger, and after passing through one or two tight corridors I eventually end up at the main entrance. And, as usual, I'm here before Alex. I

quietly count down from 5, turning to see him sprinting towards me.

"H- how?" he asks, completely out of breath. I just laugh. Right on cue.
"You didn't even pass me? What's your secret?" I gave him a simple shrug and patted his shoulder.
"A magician never reveals their secrets." he looks up at me, standing tall again.
"Maybe you have magic after all, maybe you've been able to teleport this whole time!" he pretends to act shocked, I cross my arms, unamused.
"Sorry, sorry. Sore subject huh?" he nudges my arm, laughing. I ignore him and push open the door. I know he's only joking and he knows I am too. It's just our thing, I guess.

Oh and, spoiler alert, Alex was right.

As we enter the hall. there, in big bold letters, read "The mission you've all been waiting for is finally approaching!" on the projector screen. I'm not going to live this one down. Great.
"You're just in time Alex. Take your seat." and even better! Miss Wicker is the designated speaker. Perfect. I noticed only one more seat

86

was available so I sneaked off to the side to grab a spare. I mean I know she hates me but, is putting one extra chair out really so difficult?

Once everyone has quieted down the presentation begins, and to say the least, I'm horrified. What is this? I've been training to take part in an attack! But not just any attack, a surprise attack on Ventura! My home! If I had a drink it'd be everywhere but the cup right now. I glance over at Alex, to see if he seems just as disturbed as me, but he seems to be completely drawn in. enticed. And... excited? Almost.
Miss Wicker then moves to the last slide. But the only thing on this one was a date.
"10/10/23"
It doesn't take much to understand that that's the date that this will all start. But- this can't actually be real. Where's the slide saying 'april fools' or 'get pranked'? I know others love playing jokes here, I've been the victim of plenty of them after all.
And I know these guys can be slightly hot-headed at times but...

They are my family...

I look around at everyone cheering. Something feels different, almost as if every beat my heart does, a new knife is being pushed deeper inside it. My stomach starts to turn and I feel like I'm going to throw up. I stand up, push through the crowd behind me and run to the closest bathroom. It's not like they'll notice I've run off.

After practically coughing up my insides into the sink, I look up at myself in the mirror. While splashing my face with water I notice something different from me. As if the water is slowly washing off a mask, as if I can see a little clearer with every drop. A few tears escape and race down both my cheeks.

I think I get it now…

***

I look up and wipe my eye's in the mirror. 13 days… that's how long I have. In that time I have to plan, recruit, train and save my brother. How am I going to pull this all off… obviously I don't have time to look for any more recruits so I'll probably have to just settle for the only few people I know, but they going to require much more training time.

As I pace my room, trying to come up with a plan, my door swings open.

It's Rose.

"Ash..? uh I heard sniffling... So I um... came up to see if, you know, to see if you're ok?" I don't turn around to look at her and instead just nod as I try to find my notebook, which I realise is laying upside down on the floor. I must've pushed it off the side before I passed out.
"Oh uh- well. Goodnight. I guess." Then I hear footsteps that indicate that she's walking out. But I stop her just as she's about to close the door. I just remembered, she can't be a recruit if she's mad at me, it'll make the other steps way more complicated. Plus, she's one of the strongest out of the others, I need to fix whatever is wrong. Fast.

"Wait!" I shout, she pauses in my doorway and spins around on her heel. I take in a deep breath. Come on Ash. put on that sad look. Sure, I don't know exactly what I'm about to apologise for, but as long as it fixes this gap in my plan, what's the harm?
"I... uh... I'm sorry." I sigh, acting genuine. She takes a few steps into my room and I think up something else to say. This all started after I

brought Misty home, so, maybe just apologise for that?
"I'm sorry for bringing Misty back. I shouldn't have just assumed I was allowed. I'm sorry…"
Fortunately for me, she seems to buy it. She then walks over to where I'm standing and wraps her arms around me, pulling me into a hug. The touch causes tension to course through my body.
"I forgive you Ash. It's my fault too. I should've stood up for myself more. I should've said something to you rather than just keeping it all to myself. We are friends after all."

Friends…

"Right. Well. I've got some stuff to do before bed, but it's nice to know we've fixed this." I say quickly, pulling out of her grasp. She smiles.
"Yeah. I've got some homework to do too. Goodnight, Ash. and goodnight Misty." as she exits the room she strokes Misty, who purrs and jumps up onto my desk. I sit down on my chair, wait for my door to close and open up my notebook.
That was surprisingly easy to do. That's good for me.

I continue to jot down my ideas and try to remember more from that presentation, because the more I can remember the more I can sabotage. It's all a blur, but I still try anyway. Constantly throughout the night. The time almost flew past. It's almost as if when I look down for a second I see hours have just come and gone in one single blink.
I slam down my pen and groan in frustration, which wakes Misty up. She was peacefully sleeping on my lap beforehand. She jumps up onto my book and I push her off of it.

"Misty! Move! I have to do this." I complain, leaning back in my chair and putting my hands on my forehead, which has only now started to hurt.
"Ash, go to sleep. You can continue this all tomorrow." I got out of my chair and jumped back a few steps, roughly rubbing my eyes. Am I dreaming? Did I fall asleep on top of my notebook again?
Because I'm pretty sure she just- talked?
"Ahhh! I? you? Did you? you just… spoke! To me!" she just looks up at me innocently, acting like I already knew she could do that. "Wait… is this my ability? Animal communication? Woah, it took long enough, and honestly, I was kinda hoping for something. I don't know.

More- useful?" I mean this is cool but... not at all helpful in any case scenario.
"What? No. This isn't your power." she says in a more serious tone. I blink a few times.
"Then how are you talking to me?" I'm talking to a damn cat... this has to be rock bottom.
"I'm your animal companion."
"My what?" wait.
"Your animal companion, your animal guide if you will. All powerful witches have one. We give you guidance and help you in all ways magical throughout your life. Oh and, you're the only one who can hear me, so keep that in mind when you talk to me in public." She paces my desk as she explains, I just stare at her, at a loss for words.
"S- so. Basically. you're here to help me?"
"Pretty much yes."
"But, my mother told me that you guys were only gifted to the best witches. And I'm not a witch? Let alone a powerful one." I clarify with a heavy sigh.
"Oh you silly child. Of course you're a witch! You're probably one of the strongest, but that's not a surprise, you are a spring after all. You clearly just haven't realised it yet." I can't help but laugh. Me? A witch? Pft! Sure. I've obviously just hit my head too hard on my desk or something. This is clearly not real.

"And I'm just supposed to believe a random talking cat? Alright then. Tell me what my magic ability is that is so 'powerful'." I take a seat back at my desk and cross my arms. "I can't tell you, but you already have it, and probably already know what it is. You just don't want to accept it." my mind goes blank for a second. What is she on about?

Then I feel something click... I grasp my head and groan.

"Ugh! I need to sleep. I'm clearly going crazy!" Misty follows me over to my bed. "Thank you. Go ahead to sleep Ash, everything will still be here in the morning." and that was the last thing I heard before I fell asleep.

But every minute I sleep is a minute I could spend planning. This time is valuable and I really don't have much left. I've wasted enough.

12.
I don't have time.

I'm already wide awake when Rose tells me it's time to get ready for school. I've barely gotten any sleep these past few days so waking up early really isn't an issue I have right now. I get washed, dressed and go down to the kitchen to meet her. thankfully after that little incident with Misty nothing has drastically changed at all. I mean, not that I'm bothered. Like I said before, if we didn't patch whatever it was up it would either mean we'd be too awkward around each other which would make everyone else feel uncomfortable during training and on the actual day, or I'd have to cut her from the plan entirely. But that would mean changing everything I've already done, and I really don't have that kind of time. I'm running seriously low on time as it is. So in that sense, I had to rebuild some of our new bridge. But I'm not personally bothered either way because it doesn't affect me, It only affects my team.

"Morning guys." I say as I enter the dining room. Rose and Leila were the only two in there. I haven't actually seen Mrs Paramore since that incident with Misty, not that that's a bad thing either.
"You ready to go, Rose?" I ask, quickly grabbing my bag and shoes from the chair I left them on yesterday.
"Yep, I'm ready. Just gotta finish this last sentence. I completely forgot I had homework due today." She replies with a laugh. I don't join in. Instead, I walked out into the hall and into the living room where I'd left my school project notes. Then go back and put them into my bag's front pocket.

"Ash? Are you not going to have breakfast before you leave?" Leila asks while I pack the rest of my books. "I haven't actually seen you eat anything for quite a while.." I can hear the concern in her voice but, just like sleep, food is the last thing on my mind.
"I'm fine. If I get hungry I'll just grab something on the way." I say simply.

"Ok. Do you wanna take your lunch though? I made you one a little earlier on-" I sigh and throw my head back, a little more aggressive than I originally intended, but I don't apologise.
"Fine." I take the box she was holding out and push it down under all my other clutter. She frowns but doesn't say anything, she just goes back to drinking her coffee.
"Right. Ready to go Rose?"
And with that we leave and head to school.
Was I a little rude? Maybe. But I have so many more important things to be worrying about.
The way I act towards others is not even on my back up list of things.

"So, uh. What's up with you and Leila?" Rose quizzes, not looking in my direction.
"What? Nothing. Why would you-?"
"No reason… sorry for asking. You just seemed more snappy towards her lately…"
"Have I?" It was noticeable?
"Sort of… sorry. I shouldn't be assuming." I look up and notice the school coming into view.
"Yeah. well. We're fine. I'm fine. Everythings fine." I finalise, starting to pick up my pace.

Except we aren't fine. Everything definitely isn't fine.

She doesnt catch up with me when I walk off. She instead heads over to that little clique she's still a part of. Though, I don't think they're too keen on her anymore.
No bother, I don't want her to follow me. I'm perfectly capable of walking alone.

On my walk to class I see Max and Bleu talking to Val at her locker. They call out to me but I ignore them. For all they know I'm wearing earphones and that's why I don't reply. They'll probably believe that. Everyone believed everything else I've said so far.
I just need to fly through these pointless lessons and then get back to what's actually important.

"Hey Ash! I called out your name by the lockers earlier, you probably didn't hear me." was the first thing Max said to me as he took his seat in our first lesson. I in fact did hear him. Fun fact, I actually don't know how to not hear everything around me, but I'm not about to admit that to him.
"Oh. sorry. I guess I was too into my music." I reply calmly, taking out my headphones that weren't turned on.
"That's ok! Say, would you maybe want to meet up with me, Bleu and Val after school today?

Maybe bring Rose along too?" he asks casually. I reach under the table to grab my notebook and pencil case.
"Sorry. I'm busy. But ask Rose, she's been dying to get out of the house." My voice is dull. Empty. I can't waste time laughing and talking about the most idiotic things with my team, that's not productive, but if they take Rose out then she won't be at the house to ask me so many small minded questions for a little while. It keeps her out of my way.
"Oh..? ok. That's fine. What have you got to do? Were we set homework that I don't know about?" for god's sake, what is it with everyone asking me questions today? If I'm busy. I'm busy. Why is everyone digging around me for extra information!
"No. we weren't, and what I have to do is nothing I can't handle. It doesn't matter."
"Oh... I'm sorry I wasn't-" he starts his apology but he's quickly cut off by Miss J.
Thank goodness.

The lesson is just as boring and useless as usual. Though, even if these lessons were half decent, I don't even have a magic ability anyway, and if this great magical ability Misty told me about that night was in fact real, I very much doubt that learning how to play a guitar mid-air will be of any use. I only chose this track as a cover. The others would have meant more pointless busy work. And would probably require more effort in getting out of any practical work. Bard is pretty easy to cheat through.

Once I get bored of watching the clock I open up my notebook with all my plans in and start writing in it. To the teacher I'm sure it just looks like I'm making notes, which I am, but not ones she'd approve of.
I have a section dedicated to the others, so I can properly analyse them. I write out their important, valuable qualities and things they'll need to work on later on. It's the easiest way I can select what exactly to train them on, because we don't have time to train in everything.
Unfortunately Val's page is pretty empty. I definitely need to get closer to her at some point. But for now I need to focus on the layout of the headquarters, or 'the base' which it's mostly known as. Which is such an original name I know.
I start to map it out and plan entrance and exits for when we-

"Ash? Pst. what are you doing?" I quickly slam shut my book and look up at the teacher as soon as I hear Max's voice. Avoiding eye contact with him.
"Nothing, just checking my homework." I lied. What I'm doing is not any of his business, Or at least not yet. Besides, It's my notebook. Not his.
"Oh, ok. Sorry. I was just curious. The little doodles look really cool, by the way." he whispers quickly before turning his focus back to the teacher. Little doodle? What 'little doodle'? I don't doodle. That's a waste of precious space. Space I can use for more important things, rather than useless little drawings…

I quickly flip through my notebook, scanning each page checking for any small drawing I could have subconsciously drawn, I do need all of the space in this book after all. But I scan through it multiple times and don't see anything. There's nothing here. Of course there isn't! I stopped doing that years ago. That habit was knocked out of me fast.
Ugh! I'm just being paranoid. Obviously Max was making a joke. Not that he knows any of my triggers, but the intention could have still been there…

Finally the bells ring. But it's only the end of the first lesson. I sigh and start packing up my things. I'm then interrupted by Bleu, who runs over to me with a big smile.
I'm forced to put down my stuff and look up.

"Hey Ash! Omg I feel like we haven't spoken in ages!" They complain. I force a smile. We literally spoke a few days ago.
"Yeah. well-"
"Hey Bleu? Can you come out here for a second?" I'm cut off by Max, who's calling out for his twin from the hallway. They apologise to me and run out the back door.
I think about using this to my advantage, so I grab my bag and quickly run through the other door. This door went straight into a parallel corridor so I wouldn't run into them at any point. I speed walk down the hall, straight towards the office.
I don't want to be stuck here any longer, and I don't have to be.
May as well put my fake signature skills to use.

I quickly write myself a sick note, signing it off with Mrs Paramore's signature and hand it into the office. They immediately let me go. Just like that.

People really need to stop being so gullible. Like come on. Getting away with things is getting way too easy, at least give me a little bit of a challenge.

13.
Change of plans

I call over to Bleu and guide them away from Ash. I don't know exactly what's wrong with them, but something definitely is, and I'm sure they just need a moment of peace.

"I'll be back in a sec." I hear them say before skipping over to me. I quickly pull them around the corner. "What's up?" they ask, completely oblivious.
"I think… I think Ash needs some alone time. They seem quite tired." I explained. Trying to make Ash's sudden change of mood more casual and reasonable. Bleu raises their eyebrow and tilts their head slightly.
"But they seemed ok when I spoke to them? Maybe they just need me to cheer them up. I can do that. I'm always able to cheer other

people up!" they turn around to head back into the classroom and I try to protest. I don't like to tell them what to do, but I know Bleu can get upset when their friends shut them down. And I don't think they can handle any more upsets at the moment.
I follow them into the room, but Ash has already left. I quietly sigh with relief.

"They must be racing us to the break room! Typical Ash!" They laugh. I smile softly and nod my head.
"I guess so, yeah." I don't have the heart to shoot their imagination down. I say we better get going if we wanna beat them there but Bleu stops me.
"Max! I think Ash left something behind." I spin around and see them standing in front of Ash's seat, looking down at the table.
"What?"
"Yeah, this notebook, with all the scribbles on the cover. It was in their spot." I walked over to them and picked up the book.
It's a crimson red notebook, with scuffed edges and many little doodles covering the front and the back. There's also a box on the front that's a slightly lighter shade of red that reads 'Ashley's notes' but with the 'ley' part scribbled out, with what seems to be a plain black biro,

since you can still see underneath it. Then I noticed, underneath that writing it says, in rough handwriting, 'planning journal'.
I immediately recognised it, it's the book they'd slammed shut after I asked what they were doing a little earlier on.
But they said it was homework? And this doesn't seem like it's one of our homework books.

"Let me have it. I can give it back to them! I'll guard it with my life!" they say, taking the book out of my hands and pulling a classic superhero pose. I shake away my doubts and laugh.
"Ok, super Bleu, let's safely return this precious notebook to Its rightful owner." I reply, playing along. It may seem silly to me, and everyone else, but it makes them happy, and that's what matters most.
They put the book into their backpack and we started to exit into the now not so quiet corridor. I spot Val by the windows, clearly waiting for us. I try to get her attention, grab Bleu's hand and guide them over to her.

"Hey! I've been waiting forever! What took you both so long?" she asks with a bright smile, jumping down from the window sill she was sitting on.

"Sorry, we were waiting for Ash. but they've gone on ahead of us and-"

"And they left a notebook, so I'm on a mission to return it to them!" Bleu finishes off for me.

"oh. ok, cool!" We begin to walk through the corridors to the break room in search of our friend.

"So did you ask Ash if she wanted to join us after school? And… maybe Rose too?" She tries to act cool but I've been getting pretty good at reading people, and with the way Val avoids eye contact and plays with her hair when talking about Rose, It's easy to see that she likes her.

"Uh, Ash is busy. But they said to ask Rose. something about how she's," I lift up my hands and mimic opening air quotes "dying to get out of the house." and mimic closing them.

"Ok, I'll try to find her at lunch." she says, trying to hide her burning cheeks. I try hard not to laugh. I understand sometimes having a crush is embarrassing, so I won't point it out to her. Not now anyway.

We finally reach the break room, Me and Val shift over to a corner and continue making plans for later on while Bleu goes on a hunt for Ash. I can already see they aren't here, but don't want to say anything. It doesn't take Bleu long to realise themselves and run back over to us.

"They aren't here, maybe I should-" I shake my head and cut them off unintentionally.
"Bleu, it's ok. My next class is with Ash, I can give it back to them then for you." I smile weakly as I try to reassure them. I know if I don't they'll spend the whole day trying to find them, rather than going to their classes.
"Ok... but you have to look after it!" they plead, refusing to let go of the notebook straight away. I let them put it into my backpack and promised to take good care of it.

Unfortunately I didn't see Ash in our next class, nor the classes after that. They must have just been sent home early, which would make sense. They might have been acting weird because they were sick. It's a possibility.
But the whole entire day my mind is on that notebook, tucked away in my bag. What's really in there? What 'plans' need their own clearly secret planning journal? Would it be so bad if I just took a quick peek?

No. Max. of course it would. That's obviously snooping. You can't excuse that. This is clearly personal to them. You can't dig around their notes after they've been so nice to you.
I did take the book out at lunch, considering opening it and reading a bit of it, but Val talked me out of it. But I may have dropped it back with my other books, but I didn't drop my thoughts. I couldn't figure out how too. And they only started to get worse, as if I was gradually overthinking more and more every time a minute ticked by.

Maybe they're planning something top secret, like a secret party? Or a big project for the government? Or maybe they are with a big organisation that's planning some kind of attack! Maybe a surprise attack on a kidnapper or some other kind of criminal. Or maybe they want to take away all of Ventura's magic because they don't have any of their own! Ok, Max, you're going slightly off track. It's probably just plans for different school projects for teachers or something. Come on. Ash isn't in some organisation and they definitely don't want to take over the island. You're jumping around too much with these assumptions.
But no teacher has asked them directly to do anything during lessons.

Stop it Max.

Finally, school is out. I can find Rose, pass over the notebook and forget everything. No more wild speculations.

I find Bleu at the gates, along with Val and Rose. They don't notice me straight away. I take a deep breath.

"Hey guys!"
"Hey Max! Did you give Ash the book back? Did you say I found it for them?" Bleu immediately blurts out as soon as they notice I'm here. I scratch the back of my neck out of habit.
"Book? What book?" Rose quickly adds in.
"Oh, when we went to get Ash, we couldn't find them, but they left behind a red notebook. I haven't been able to find them since to give it back." My hands danced as I explained the situation to Rose and answered Bleu's question. I reached into my bag and showed her the book.
Maybe she knows what it's for. Maybe she can shoot down my thoughts for me.
"Oh, I don't think I've seen that before.." she starts but takes a moment to think afterwards.

"Wait- no! I have seen that on their desk a few times before, and I've seen them writing a few times when I've gone up to tell them something, but everytime they slam it shut. I never really pay too much attention but I definitely know it was that book. It's kinda hard to mistake." I look down at the notebook, taking in how damaged and worn down it is. I bet they've probably had it for a while.
"Now that I think of it, they've been writing in their room a lot, definitely more than usual these past few days." we all pause for a moment, probably all feeling the same sort of feeling.
"Is it bad that… I feel kind of suspicious?" Val asks, sighing and lowering her head. I shake mine.
"No. I'm the same. Something just doesn't feel right." I admit, feeling a little better now I know I'm not the only one. feeling like this has felt wrong. Ash is my best friend, they have been nothing but nice to me, and I trust them… usually. Because right now, for some reason, I'm doubting my trust, and I hate it. But I feel validated by the fact I'm not alone…

"Maybe we should… take a little look? You know, just the first page?" Val suggests carefully. We all look at each other. Rose and

Bleu seem unsure. "There might be a title or something on there, it might tell us what's in there. Then if it's nothing to worry about, we just act oblivious. Yeah?" she adds. I mean, what harm could that do? It's not like we're reading the entire thing. If it's something simple or something for someone we can just turn a blind eye, pretend we had no idea. I look around at everyone and we all collectively agree. Even Bleu.
What could go wrong?

14.
Oh...

I reach the Paramore's house only half an hour after I leave. It didn't take me as long to walk since it was just me. It's shocking how productive you can be when you're alone, even with dangerously low energy levels.
I try swiftly slipping in and up to my bedroom but unfortunately, Leila spots me. Of course. Just my luck.

"Hey Ash! Wait. Ash? School definitely isn't over yet. Has it? Did I miss an email?" She pulls out her phone and starts scrolling. I push past her and head towards the second staircase.
"No. You didn't. I was just feeling sick. They sent me home early." I lie, trying to get up to my room, but she stops me.

"Wait! your sick? I knew something was up! Are you ok? Do you need anything?" Her eyes soften up as she looks at me. She tries to grab my hand but I pull away. I turn and walk up the stairs.
"I'm fine. Just gotta rest" I groan in annoyance.
"Ok.. well I'll bring up your meals for you, so you don't have to get up and walk about. And I'll bring you some water too, Since I know that's all you drink now, and if you need anything else just call me. Ok?" She shouts up at me. Now that I'm out of sight I roll my eyes. She can do what she wants, it doesn't mean I have to do what she wants. it's ok though, Misty will probably very happily eat and drink whatever she brings up. I really can't waste time on that stuff. I can't stress enough how important other things are. The future of Ventura literally depends on these things! My own needs can wait.

Why doesn't anyone understand?

Well they will. they will all understand. Once everythings ready to be public they'll know and will stop pestering me with questions. And I'll finally get to stop lying...
I guess, Not that it matters. I can lie forever if I have to. It's for their own good afterall.

The sound of my door closing obviously wakes Misty up and, while I go to reach for my notebook, she wanders over to me.
"Ok. I know I'm just a cat but, I'm pretty sure you shouldn't be here." She tilts her head slightly to the right.
"What! No, I am!" I say dramatically, pretending to act hurt. It takes her a moment to realise that I'm joking. I chuckle, dropping my bag.
"Ash! You can't just skip school! you-"
"I what? Seriously. Why do I actually have to go to school? It's not like I have any magical ability!" I snap, My blood boiling. She jumps back from me when my voice raises. I sigh and fall down into my chair, I start feeling dizzy but ignore it. It settle's after a while.
"But you do and you know that." she uses my lap to jump onto my desk.
"But I don't! I don't know!" I throw up my hands to my head, sweeping my hair out of my face with my fingers. My hair falls off to the side and I can see more clearly now.
Misty looks up at me and tilts her head. I give her a confused expression.
"What?"
"That."
"What? Is there something on my face or-?" I ask, wiping at my left cheek.

"No. your eye. Ash." Then I remember.
"Yes. It's a funky colour. I know. So what." I groan, rolling my eyes and leaning back in my chair. She doesn't say anything else. She just stares at me. I start to get a little uncomfortable. What could she be-? Wait.
"Hold on. You're not saying? No. nope. It's not-" I shake off quickly, but she stays staring at me. And although she's not saying anything, It's like I know what she's thinking. I get up and walk off into the bathroom. She unfortunately follows.
"I know you know Ash. you can't keep shutting it out." I place my hands on the edges of the sink, looking down, away from the mirror.
"Ash you are-"

"No! I'm not!" I yell, finally looking up. The first thing I notice is my eye. The eye that is now… glowing? I look around me and notice the room getting brighter and brighter by the second. I tighten my grip on the sink, squeeze my eye's shut, causing tears to trickle down. The room starts getting louder, I even hear Misty scream. I start crying. outloud. What is happening? Why does it hurt?

"Ash! Calm down! Breathe!" How did I hear that in the muffled noise? I don't know. But I did. I loosen my grip, move one hand to my chest and try to steady my breathing. wincing from the pain every now and again. It takes a while, but once the sounds calm down, so do I. I take back control of my body again and gradually start to open my eyes. Then I realise exactly what has happened. The room is completely destroyed, almost every inch of the room is completely scorched! I jump back from the now burnt sink, put out a few fire sparks and look for Misty in the rubble.

"Oh my god- Misty! Misty!" I call out frantically, rummaging through everything.
"Misty! haha- this isn't funny! Come on! Cut it out!" The longer I spent trying to find her the more tears I was unable to stop. I start to tell myself that she's gone, that it's useless looking. But then, just as I'm about to leave the room, a certain black kitten jumps out from behind the cupboards, a little bit of her fur burnt. I chase after her, lift her up, and hold her close, crying desperately into her fur.
"Oh my god! Mi pequeña bebé! I thought I lost you!" I cry, she brushes off her burnt patch.
"No no. I'm fine. Your magic can't hurt me" My eyes widen, I hold her at arm's length and stare at her.
"Wait? I, I did this? I have…"

"Magic? Yeah. I have been trying to tell you." I take her back into my bedroom, where everything is still intact, and sit us on the bed. "So... I do have magic..." I sigh, looking down at my hands. This is what I've wanted, I've been waiting for this moment all my life. But now that it's actually here, I feel uneasy. Unsteady. I'm starting to feel like I don't quite know myself after all...
"Yeah. and very powerful magic at that."
"Pft! Yeah. I just burnt down my whole goddamn bathroom." I say sarcastically. "Sorry. Force of habit..." I pause.
"But why? Why do I have this? Why is it so powerful?" my mind is racing, way faster than it's ever raced before.
"People believe there are many reasons witches are given more powerful abilities. Sometimes it's 'because they've been trusted, by the universe, to hold the great power. To keep it safe and under control and out of the reach of others who'd use it for evil.' or Some are given it 'because it's fate, their destiny, almost. Because they're destined to do something great.' but it's actually passed down. If a bloodline is known to be very powerful, it's likely the bloodline stays powerful. Though, the longer that line goes on for, the more likely it is

that the power will die out. For example, your family's bloodline."
"My bloodline was… my ancestors were all powerful?" scratch not 'quite' knowing who I am. I feel like I don't know myself at all!
"Yes. extremely! Did your parents never tell you?" I look over at her, shaking my head.
"Your ancestors were the founders of Ventura. You're a direct descent of them. This city you've lived in for most of your life is literally named after your family! Anyway, the island blessed your family with great power, all because of their strong family bond, and then, after they started to build up their home, other people started moving here too, and whoever was born on the island's soil was granted one single magical ability, but only your family was directly given power greater than anything else! So actually, anyone else who has slightly more powerful abilities, probably has a little bit of your bloodline running through them, but that's very rare." as she begins to explain, I try pinching my arm, just to make sure I'm actually awake. This feels too much like a dream.
"That… that's… something..." I stammer in disbelief. What exactly am I supposed to do with this information?
"I'm sure your parents would've told you. They were probably just waiting for the right time."

her voice goes slightly soft, maybe because she knows she'll rub an open wound if she's not careful. But, I never told her why my parents aren't here?
I feel like I should say something, but I can't bring myself to do so. So I just threw out another question. It was better than the defining silence, and I may as well find out all I can now, rather than pounder.

"So? did I just get my power now?" I ask, standing up and pacing my room.
"No. You've had it for a while actually." wait? So I've had a magic ability and just never knew? I stop pacing to look at Misty.
"when- when exactly did I get it then? I must've known something was off. There's no way I wouldn't have noticed something as big as that!" I say, pointing over to the bathroom. I definitely would've noticed if something like that had happened before.
"Uh- I- I shouldn't say-"
"Oh. No. You have to tell me." I clarify "you can't drop bombshells on me without explanations! I at least deserve to know when this started."
"I mean, it really doesn't matter when-"
"no. It really matters. It matters more now that you're clearly avoiding telling me!" I raise my

119

voice a little, in some type of way of showing that I'm serious. I have to know. I must know. And I will know.

"Uh... well... Your eye!" she then shouts, pointing her right paw to my eye. My eyebrow raises. What about my eye? "When did you get it?"
"I don't know. I've always had it..?" I say, crossing my arms and standing tall. She's just trying to change the topic.
"No you haven't. Your eye changed colour the day you got your ability." wait what?
"But that doesn't answer my question then. Because I don't know when I got this! I've always had it." I sigh, pacing once again, this time out of annoyance. I can't remember a time when I had two matching eyes. One has always been different. At least, for as long as I can remember.
"ugh! Why can't I just remember!" I cry out, Flopping down on my bed in frustration. Misty climbs onto my chest and I lean back on my arms.
"well... if you really want to know... I guess I could show you?" I sit up as she starts to emit a subtle yellow glow. What the-?
"I can take you down memory lane. If that's what you want?" she holds out her paw, as if

telling me to take it. I take a moment to consider. Sure, this is weird and probably dangerous, and I might be walking into somewhere in my past I don't want to go back to. But at the same time, I'll get answers. And that's all I want. Answers to who I am. And why.

So I hold onto her paw.

15.
For you.

Everything suddenly goes pure white, I'm assuming we are teleporting somewhere. Where? That's a good question. Could be anywhere. I almost feel like we're moving, but my eyes are closed, so I'm not sure.

"Ok, we're here." That's when I opened my eyes and realised all my worrying was for nothing. we're just at the beach. Why are we at the beach?
"Uh- the beach?"
"Yes. but 6 years into the past." Misty is floating beside me. We both have a faint yellow glow to us.
"But why?" I quiz. I don't get a verbal answer. She just simply turns and points with her paw. I copy her movements, trying to spot what she's pointing out. Then I see… me? And Rose, Leila, My parents and… Alex.

"I, I remember this day.." I say slowly, approaching my past self. I seem so... Happy. "This was the day... the day before-" my hands start to shake, so I stop and shake off the thoughts. "Why are we here?" I ask seriously, trying to ignore myself and my brother. "Look at yourself. Your eye." She insists, turning me back around. Then everything around us freezes, as if Misty had paused time. I ignore it and look over at my face. Specifically my right eye. Which was... Brown? Ok. no. This can't be right.

"Wait but that doesn't make any sense! Because after this, we. I. I definitely had it! This has to be a joke. You're playing with me right?" I ask, awkwardly laughing. Surely this is wrong. I mean, can I really trust a talking cat? "Unfortunately, this is real. I would never lie to you Ash..." I take a moment to look at myself. None of this is making any sense. Unless... "Hold on... If my eye is normal here, but was yellow when I left... Does that mean?" My thoughts start running, I can't focus on any of them. Misty nods. I grasp a hold of my head. "No. No No. but, but that doesn't make any sense. I don't remember anything happening that day, not magic related anyway. I think I'd remember if-" I start to spiral and Misty attempts to calm me down.

"I did tell you you wouldn't want to know..." She reminds me softly. she watches as I drop down to the floor.

"But that can't be! Please tell me this is all a coincidence" I cry, praying that there is an easy, obvious solution to all of this, praying that Misty will explain it all to me and It would all make sense. But the more I try to tell myself that, the less certain I seem to become.

"Let me show you... you have to know now. That's the only way you'll be able to get over it." She says, placing her paw on my shoulder. I try to protest, but it doesn't work. I don't have a choice. I don't have a say in this. As much as I don't want to relive that day, I have to. Misty was right on that. I need to know.

After a gush of wind passes, I open my eyes, which are sore and heavy, and take in where we are.

We're on a high cliff, overseeing a long winding road on the side. I swallow hard, Mindlessly fidgeting with my hands, Watching cars fly past.

"Where are we?" I whisper, I'd speak louder if I could.
"Don't you remember?"
"Oh I remember… but that didn't happen here. I'd recognise it if it were." I clarify. I can picture almost exactly where we were that day. This definitely isn't it.
"We're as close as we can be. Your magic may not be able to hurt us, but it can blind us. And things get pretty bright." I raise an eyebrow, then go to question, but I'm distracted by a very familiar car driving along the road, which is calmer now. I run over to the cliff's edge and scream down to it but get reminded that they can't hear me. I wipe my cheeks and brace myself, knowing what's going to happen.

My eye's follow the completely defenceless vehicle down the road, then I'm passed a pair of sunglasses. I look at them and back at Misty.

"I'd put these on if I were you." With a sigh, I accepted the offer, putting them over my eyes. Everything is a lot darker now, but I can still see. The car is the only thing on the road, that is until a rather loud truck turns onto the road. It passes the car, not even grazing it. Wait what? That's not what-

The next thing I know, a huge bright ball of light grows around the car, quickly consuming the entire vehicle. It then catches a hold of the truck. I jump back and squint my eyes. The ball continues to expand rapidly, eating at the road and the mountain beside it. Then it starts to move. It edges closer and closer to the cliff. Clearly following the car... following me.
The light, as well as both vehicles, fall off the side and crash into the rocks a few feet below. That's when it started dying down, now there's a giant burnt patch on the road and hill, with two scorched cars helplessly laying upside down below it. I start to cry, louder and more freely this time. I fall to my knees and grip ahold of the earth.

I did this...?

"Take my paw..." Misty says quickly, probably because she's sick of seeing me crying, at my lowest. Probably fed up of seeing me crumble into a million pieces. I get it. I understand.

I'm showing weakness. I'm showing emotion. And I shouldn't be. Crying into the past soil beneath me is doing absolutely nothing. I'm not gaining anything, just embarrassing myself. I'm just reliving past events, crying over things I've

already shed so many tears on, wishing wishes I've already recited, praying for things that aren't possible.
In my head, I know this is stupid. I can't go back. I can't change anything. I can't go down a different path, or rebuild my old one. I know all of this.
But there's something inside me... something that's making me feel something else. Something is making me feel things I never have before... regret? sadness? grief? Sorrow maybe? I can't place it. I can't label it. The only thing that I know is that I hate it.

I force myself up and hold onto Misty's paw, feeling so many different things, my mind has become too overwhelmed. She teleports us back to the present, back into my bedroom. I wait for the yellow glow to fade, then I sink into my bed.

"So... I survived because... because it was my magic that caused everything?" I question, feeling helpless. I stare up at the ceiling as I talk. Feeling as if the weight of this blame is pinning me down.
"sort of. Even though it was caused by your magic, you could have still died from the impact after the car fell off the cliff."

"Hold on?" I push myself out of my slump to look at her. "So, you're telling me that, I killed my parents and just happened to live! Completely due to pure luck!" It gets harder and harder to speak through the tears, but I push through anyway. "Why didn't I die! I was the cause of all of this! I'm the reason they died!"

"Because you have things to do, to accomplish. Your story wasn't ready to end!" I jump up and start to pace, ignoring her words. For a moment, anyway.

"Besides, you were only 9! You had no idea you-"

"So that makes everything ok!" I groan, annoyed. Feeling my blood boiling. "I killed my parents, but it's all ok! Because I was just a child! And because I didn't know? They're dead! Because of me! Do you know what that means?"

"Well yes but-"

"Oh my god! What is Alex going to think! He missed out on the rest of his childhood all because of me! Mami and Papi should be here, With him! But they aren't... And I'm to blame for everything!" I cover my face, hiding myself from the world. This place doesn't need me. I'm nothing more than a murderer.

My parents should be here. Not me. They should be raising my brother to be the best he can be. They should be visiting my grave, telling me about their adventures, or telling me about the new person they've met, or the new show they've watched in memory of me. Not the other way around!

"Ash. I know it may seem like everyone would be better off if you were in your parents palace-"

"Wait, how did you-?"

"But trust me. It wouldn't be. These things just happen, whether you want them to not. And we shouldn't spend our lives wishing the island had taken us instead. Everything happens for a reason. And sure, acceptance takes time. But trust me. It was not just a matter of luck! You're here for a reason!" My stomach starts to ache while a large lump forms in my throat. I feel like everything has just started individually spinning, I can't focus on anything.

"No! Stop! I can't do this!" I yell, running out of my room and slamming the door shut behind me. I slowly slide down the closest wall, drowning myself in my own living nightmare. I'm sitting still but everything is still moving. My breathing is heavy and my vision blurry, and it is for a while. I almost feel as if this is it, my end. I think of how the conversation with my brother would go, his fiery blasts hit me over and over, His words stabbing me while his expressions push me around, my head crashing into every existing wall. It's as if I've turned into a small fly on the wall, flying around, looking for a way out while being swatted by everyone I love.

I sit through all these hallucinations. Scared to do anything, to say anything. But then I remember, these are just that. Hallucinations. I try my hardest to wake myself back up. It takes a few minutes but it does work. It's as if, through all the chaos, I saw a little light. A light guiding me through all of the mess. I suddenly knew exactly how to free myself. Because, no matter how bad these things seem, they aren't real. Not yet. I can get myself out of them. Because now that I know, I can fix it. I can prevent these things from becoming reality. Sure, I can't change what I've done, but I can change the rest, I have the chance to turn onto a new road, a chance to edit my ending. The light starts fighting against the mist, brightening up my path some more. I push and push and eventually reach my body. I lift up my head, which starts to get lighter, and slowly get back onto my feet.

"I've got to be the reason. Not the blame."

The more I repeat it in my head the easier everything gets. I almost laugh my mood off.

I push open my door and walk over to my window. Misty is asking me questions but I block her out. I just close my eyes, lean against the glass, then look up at the clouds. I take in a few deep breaths, making sure I'm truly back.

"Maybe I can't change my past, I can't bring back my parents and I can't our switch places. But I know they're looking down on me, and they're probably beating themselves up over the fact that they've left me like this. I don't want to think of them doing that anymore." I say simply, looking over at Misty who's sat up proudly. "I guess I should stop crying, for them, and start fixing what I've done…" I finished playing with my necklace. Misty nods her head. "I know you've got this Ash. You're a lot stronger than you think" I force a smile, heading over to her for a hug, but then I hear Rose's voice calling for me. I sigh, but not out of annoyance.
"Give me a second, Rose needs me downstairs." My voice is light, and my

expression is soft. I call down to her, calmly make my way down the stairs and through the corridors until I reach the dining room.

I'm smiling as I enter, but struggle to maintain it once I spot Bleu, Max, Rose, Val and Leila all scattered around the room, with multiple negative expressions shared out between them all. I open my mouth and ask everyone what was wrong,

then I see it...

16.
Not what it looks like

"Hey! Uh- what's up?" I ask, mindlessly, as I enter the dining room. But after a small scan of the room, I noticed it...

My notebook, in the centre of the table.

I swallow hard, Immediately replacing my walls and preparing myself.

"Hmm. I don't know. We just found this notebook. I believe it belongs to you?" Val spits, stepping closer to me, however Rose pulls her back away.
"I... I don't know what-" I see all their stares and decide to shut up. Clearly they've read through it. I jump towards the table, grab the

book, and jump back to the doorway. Holding it close.
"You shouldn't have gone through it! It doesn't say your name on the cover now does it? That's snooping for god's sake!"
"And you shouldn't be judging us! Writing out our strong and weak points, criticising our traits!" Rose remarks, her response was quick, as if she knew what I was going to say, as if she'd been practising her comebacks for a while. I sigh loudly.
"I had to." I reply in a low whisper. For what feels like the first time, I'm unsure on what to say. Normally It's easy for me to get out of things like these, but this time, for some reason, I can't think of an escape. I'm still not ready to tell them the truth, but I guess I don't really have a choice now. I hug my notebook close to my chest, rubbing the back where my brother had signed it, while taking a deep breath.

You got this Ash.

"We thought we were your friends…" I hear Max croak.
"You picked us all up, brought us together…" Val mutters afterwards.

"We took you in, gave you a home..." Rose adds. Bleu goes to say something but I cut them off. Accidentally.

"I never asked for anything from any of you! You didn't have to even talk to me!" I shout out. If they didn't want me, then why did they give me their hands?
"Because we were your friends! That's what friends do!" I then notice they all have watery eyes. I try standing my ground, but something inside me is telling me that they're right, so I take a step back.
"We opened our hearts to you... but you opened your notebook..." Bleu finally says, playing with one of their keychains. Max wraps an arm around their shoulder.

"But you don't understand! I had to!" My defence is weak, sure, but it's there. I needed to find people for my team and I couldn't worry them. I had to think fast, I really didn't have much time! What was I supposed to do instead? It's the only thing I could think of! And there was no way that I could've told them before this point! I'd just left my home, I needed to learn to walk on my own two feet before I ran.

"Why! What's so important that requires you to judge your friends in secret!" Rose points at me while she takes a few steps closer. Her finger is almost touching my face. I push her back, gently, but with enough force to move her.
Wait did they-? Did they not read the other pages?
"so... you guys only read the pages about yourselves? You didn't read the others?" If they haven't read through the rest of my planning, maybe I can get myself out of this hole after all!
"Well no. We flicked through the first few pages, but only read the pages with our names in bold letters!" Val says sharply, running her fingers through her hair, which was falling in her face.
"So you guys have no idea why! Of course! Because you surely wouldn't be standing here yelling at me if you did!" I laugh, dropping my hands to my sides, standing just a little bit taller as my strength returns.
"Ok. So tell us. Why?" Max states boldly.
"There's a large organisation, stationed on the edge of Ventura. Their planning on invading the island. I found this out and had to build up a resistance! But I couldn't go around telling everyone then, I wasn't ready to go public, but I was going to, eventually." As I explain, I

expected for their expressions to change, and they do, but not to what I wanted them to. "So you want us to believe you're actually, secretly, planning on defeating some big organisation that wants to take over our island. But no one actually knows anything about said organisation, except for you, A powerless 15 year old? Not only that, but they put a powerless 15 year old that can't even lie properly in charge of all this! Come on Ash. that's so pathetic!" Val's words and cold voice cause my body to start heating up. "Just admit you're a bully who is too insecure about themselves so you judge everyone around you! It just makes you feel better because in reality you're just a sad, lonely teen that has no magical ability or family-"

That's all I needed to explode.

"For your information! I do have magic! Powerful magic at that! Not that that's any of your business!" The more I yell, the angrier I get. But it's only when I notice the space around me starting to light up that I realise just how angry I am, but I'm not going to calm myself down. She went too far. "And sure, I may not have a family like yours, all prissy and happy, but weren't you ever taught never to

talk ill of the dead!" I start to approach Val as I talk, growing hotter and hotter by the minute, my power being fueled by my rage.
"My familia was perfect! Amazing! They cared for me, they loved me-!"
"Ok. Ash, calm down... Ash!"
"But yes, they're gone. Dead! And is that my fault? Most likely. But you do NOT get to say anything about my familia! Especially since you know nothing about them! You know nothing about me!" Me and Val are now face to face, hers being lit up by my eye. I can feel the tension. My breathing is heavy, and I go to say more, but then I hear the others voices.

"Ash! Stop!" the others cry out. they're... frightened? They sound genuinely scared...
I close my eyes, take a few steps back, and try to calm myself down. Almost out of nowhere, an old childhood lullaby starts playing in my head, I try to focus on the words, on the voice singing it to me. And I eventually calmed down. When I open my eyes I'm met with everyone else's on me, open wide from fear. I don't even let them say anything. I leg it up to my bedroom. They might have shouted after me. I'm not sure. But If they did, they probably just wanted to accuse me of more. I've had enough of that. I've had enough of everything! They

can keep their accusations and questions to themselves. I don't want or have to speak with any of them.

I'm leaving.

17.
Everyone agrees.

I barge into my room, my anger showing in every movement. Misty tries to stop me, but I push her aside. I'm leaving, and no one is stopping me. Not that I expect anyone to. They all clearly hate me now. But what else is new. It's not like I'm a stranger to this feeling. They aren't the first to hate me, and probably won't be the last. They'll probably be happier once I'm out of their hair.

"Ash. stop! What are you doing?"
"Can't you see? I'm leaving. I can figure everything out myself. I don't need to be here any longer." I try to hide the inevitable pain in my voice. What's the point of me being here? Besides, I stole enough money that day to accommodate myself for a while. I'll figure it out. I always do.

I carelessly start chucking my basic necessities into a suitcase, my tears dampening each item. I can't fit everything, but I don't need everything. I zip it up, wipe away my stray tears and turn for the door. Misty reluctantly jumps onto my shoulder. We went to leave but someone is now standing in between me and the exit.
And it's the last person I expected.

"Ash... please don't leave." She plea's. I drop the case's handle and cross my arms.
"I'm leaving. Leila. Clearly no one here wants me around. If they did, they would have run after me" I remark bluntly. My voice is completely hollow.
"They're just upset, Ash, this really hurt them. But that doesn't mean they don't want you here. I know they don't hate you that much, nor do I..." I just roll my eyes.
"They've had time to think, and they've chosen to leave me, so I'll leave them." If they truly wanted me to stay, they'd have said something. Everyone knows that.
"But you've only just come up here-"
"Well it's not that hard. It's a yes or no question. Either they want me here or they don't." My voice raises in volume, informing her that I'm getting annoyed.

"It's not that easy Ash. These things take more time for some people."
"Well I really don't have that kind of time."
"But, even if they don't want you to stay. Won't you stay for me? I don't want to lose you. I can't lose my best friend again…" I notice her eye's starting to shimmer. Why are people so emotional?
"I don't really see much point in staying for-"
"Seriously? You won't stay for me but you'd stay for them if they had asked! Ash! I'm standing right here, practically begging you to stay! Which is what you just said you wanted the others to do! I'm your best friend! Your amiga! Am I really not a good enough reason?" her face flashes with anger. I'm confused but match her energy anyway. "I thought you were dead! Do you know what that did to me? You have no idea how I felt through those years! And when I found out you were alive- I was so happy. I thought 'oh my god! They're alive! We can go back to how we were before! Back when we were kids. When we were happy!' but I was clearly wrong. Very wrong…" Her strong posture falters and she softens back up. But instead of crying, she shows no emotions, like she's just been completely drained of all feelings. I grab a hold of the suitcase handle again, tighten my grip, push past her to reach

the doorway. Then I stop, keeping my body straight, looking the opposite way to her.

"We aren't children. We've changed. We've grown up." I simply point out. Showing no emotion myself. But as I say the words, they still taste sour. Bitter.
"Clearly." Was all she said. That was the last thing I heard her say. I walk off and head for the front door, Misty still on my shoulder. She's still telling me to reconsider but we both know I won't. I've made up my mind.

As I slam the door shut, I feel something change inside me. Or as though I'm missing something, like I know I've left something. I can't exactly say what, but something is definitely not right. I'd like to think It's something negative, proving my sudden decision was the right one.
But somehow I know I'm wrong. Whatever I've lost. Was probably something I needed. But I'll survive without it. So I don't turn back.

After a few hours of walking we came across a hotel, a few miles away from the nearest village. Misty sighs with relief in my ear as we start to walk up to it, jumping down from my shoulder.

"Finally! My paws are in so much pain!" I roll my eyes. She has barely walked anywhere. She was quite happy sleeping across my shoulders as if she were a scarf. And if she wasn't on my shoulders, she was in my bag, poking her head out and telling me random facts about the places we passed. The only time she actually stood on her own was when she was waiting for me outside a petrol station. I laugh. Then she goes to hide in my jacket just before entering the building.

"Hello Ma'am! how may I help you?" The title makes me slightly uncomfortable but I really don't feel in the mood to correct a stranger. I instead force a smile and match her energy. "Hola! I was just wondering if you had any available rooms?" While she checks her computer I grab my purse and flick through my notes. I'm sure I have enough for a little while. I've got more in my bag, but grabbing out a whole bag of cash probably isn't a very good idea if I want to look casual.
"We have a few rooms, yes, are you with anyone else? Maybe a partner? Friends? Parents?" she tilts her head, obviously expecting someone else to walk in. I want to

scoff, I know I don't quite look like an adult, but she doesn't know my age.
"No, it's just me. A single room would be fine" I reply casually, trying to stay calm.
"Oh? Ok dear. I'll look into that for you, how old are you?" she doesn't look up when she asks, but I can tell what she's thinking. She's judging me, I can hear the tone in her voice, It's changed. She's probably assuming I'm some run away child, who left after my parents took away my phone, or maybe my dessert, and this is how I chose to retaliate. And yes, I did run off, and I'm a minor, but I'm not an idiot.
"I'm 18. I'd pass over my ID but it's in my car." she nods as I recite my number plate, which was simply a plate I read a few blocks away. Just in case."so, how much will it cost?"
"Well one night in our single rooms are £50's each, that is including food and drinks-" I casually pick out two £50 notes, pass them over calmly. She looks at me for a minute, but takes them despite her clear suspicions.
"2 night's will be fine. Gracias." She hands me my room key and goes back to whatever she was doing before. I grab my suitcase and head up to my room, which is, thankfully, quite high up and out of the way. Meaning coming into contact with anyone is pretty rare, plus no one can hear me 'talk to myself'.

The room was small, but sufficient. It's separated into a sort of living room area and a bedroom with a door, which I'm assuming leads to a bathroom, by the bed. I let Misty out of my jacket pocket and inspected everything closer while she typically heads straight for the bed.
The sofa is plain with blue pillows on either end, The TV isn't big but a decent size considering the price, the windows are pretty big but there aren't very many, they do thankfully have blinds on each of them. I then enter the bedroom, checking the thickness of the walls.

"Why are you playing detective Ash? It's just your average hotel room." Misty interrupts my thinking so I stop and turn in her direction. "Because, Miss Wicker has most likely sent tropes out to look for me by now and we aren't that far from their base, so I need to be more careful now. I'm simply trying to make sure I'm not caught." I explain with a stern expression, I don't even want to think about what they'd do to me if they found me. I can't afford to let my guard down, not even for a second, if I assume I'm safe I'll be dragged by my feet all the way back to the beginning.

"Oh, that's why you only paid for 2 nights. We're gonna be moving around a lot, aren't we?"

"Exactly. But not for too long. I plan to be prepared and read within the next week." I start to count how many days I have left on my fingers. It's the 31st now, the invasion is on the 10th, Meaning i have 9 days, or 216 hours, to prepare.

"Ready for what exactly?" I resume my inspections as I run through my plan.

"To free my brother. I'm not leaving him there. I can't fight against my own familia now can I?" I need to free him from that place, we should be fighting on the same side, I can't imagine seeing him on the opposite end of the battlefield. Obviously he couldn't come with me when I escaped, I had no idea what I was doing, but I promised I'd return for him, and I will not break that promise!

"So you're telling me, we're just hiding away from these people, just to later break into their base. all for your brother?" She seems shocked. I thought this was obvious? Did she think I'd just be running and hiding the rest of my life? Hiding away and watching my home slowly get taken over by my adoptive family? Does she not know me at all? I thought she was supposed to know me better than anyone, isn't that her whole point? I thought she could tap into my thoughts for crying out loud!

"Yeah. obviously. But we'll be more prepared then. I'll make sure of it. I won't rest until I know we are 100% ready." thinking I've justified my cause well, I spin around and start going through my clothes. I find a pair of penguin pyjamas, match them with some slippers and go to change.

"Ok. But let me train you, teach you how to use your magic first." I freeze, stopping dead in my tracks. I don't face her.
"I've gotten this far without my magic. I don't need it." I finished, speaking in a 'duh' tone. I head into the bathroom and change, trying my hardest to ignore her.
"But your days away from throwing yourself into a goddamn war!" I roll my eyes. Why is she so dramatic? She sounds like the others.
"You will need your magic. Or at the least, let me teach you how to control it so you don't burn down any more bathrooms."
"I said no! Ok? I don't want anything to do with my ability!" My sudden change in volume scared both of us, but it finished the conversation. I don't know what she isn't understanding. I don't want to use my magic.

Isn't that a good enough reason? I've survived so much! Every rock life has thrown at me, I've smashed without any magical assistance. I surely can carry on without them. And besides, half of those rocks were caused by my magic!

That night I struggled to sleep. By 2 o'clock I was pacing the room, thinking of strategies and how to enter the base itself. But then I started spiralling, thinking of all the possibilities that would make this so much more difficult. For example, what if they changed the codes? Or adjusted the structure? Or moved the barracks? Or removed certain exit's or entrances? They could've had a complete makeover! Meaning all my passcodes and layouts are completely useless! Everything I've written and drawn would need to be thrown and remade! Meaning I'll be forced to jump back to square one!

Yeah. a lot was keeping me up...

I decided to stop pacing and sit on the chair by the window, repositioning it so I can look out easier. After a while, I noticed the roof directly underneath the window, that I had learnt was opened by being lifted, was flat. The drop was almost nothing. So without much thought, I

lifted up the window until I could fit out of it, collected a few pillows and blankets and laid them outside. I sat on top and looked up at the sky, feeling my mind starting to calm down. The wind was calm, the sky clear and the temperature cool. I just admire the beauty of the night. The stars scattered across the sky, the yellow balls of lights marking the streets, the quiet sounds of occasional crickets and owls. I take it all in slowly, completely forgetting why I was so stressed before. Looking at everything now, it's as if there was never anything wrong. That everything is peaceful and safe. Which is how it should be...
Ventura, the island of fortune and peace, is somewhere people move to for safety, for new beginnings, fresh starts. And the island has maintained such an extraordinary title for centuries, yet it's all going to be destroyed... unless I put a stop to it. People are here for security, for protection, and I'm not about to let others take that away from them. Because no one should ever feel unsafe in their own home...

I take a few deep breaths, close my eyes and lean back on my arms. My body starts to feel warmer, but this temperature is comfortable. Before whenever my body heated up, I felt like

I was hovering over a raging flame, but this? This is different. It feels like when you light a campfire on a cold winter night, and you sit around it, embracing the heat from a safe distance.
I start to slowly relax. I don't even care to think over why I'm feeling like this. I don't care. I don't care about anything right now. I've never felt this light before, and now that I feel it, I don't want to stop feeling it.
When I go to open my eyes again, I notice a slight yellow glow to me. But it doesn't scare me. I don't even choose to ignore it, instead I try to embrace it. I wouldn't say I like it, but I won't say that I hate it.

My magic may now be working, but after years of feeling out of place without it, I'm now thinking I can go the rest of the way without it. It shouldn't decide my worth, as if I were nothing before I started glowing and burning things down. I finally come to terms with who I truly am, and then my 'non existing' powers come and say hi? Giving me a whole other thing to worry about, a whole new thing to sort out? To fix? No thank you.

I lay on my back and look up at the stars, thinking of absolutely nothing. Well, until I notice a pair of stars shining a little brighter. And maybe it's magic, or maybe I'm just hallucinating again, either way, it's as if it was giving me a message. I sigh.

"Don't worry, Mami, Papi. I'll bring Alex home, restore peace and everything will be fixed… I won't let this second chance go to waste, I won't let this pass over my head. I'll fight for you, for him, for myself…"

18.
Winning and losing

It's the next day and I decide to take a walk around the nearby village. Misty is back in the hotel, for an immortal magic kitten she sure sleeps a lot! But I could use some alone time, so I'm not too bothered. I start walking around with my headphones playing some song I can't quite place the name of.

I glance at my phone screen and read the time. 12:30. It was a little later than I thought. I look around and spot a cafe. I'm not really in the mood for food but I can probably do with a drink, so I approach the building and push open the door, ringing the bell above it. I choose the last empty table and wait patiently for a server.

"Buenos días señora. What can I get you today?" I stare at the menu on the table in front of me as I reply.

"Could I have a glass of orange juice and a chicken sandwich por favor?" My head is still hanging low but I can see her jotting down my order. I don't want the sandwich but I feel awkward just ordering juice. Misty will probably enjoy the snack when I return anyway.
"Ok, Is that all for you today?"
"Sí, gracias." And then she skips back to the kitchen. I start to hear faint whispers behind me and I get a sudden urge to turn around, but I don't. I could have translated what they were saying wrong. It's probably not about me. They're is probably others with curly black hair around here. I just need to lay low and keep moving. Staying in any place, especially a public place, for too long Is extremely risky.
I pull out my phone, thank the waitress when she passes over my food, and try to ignore the stares and whispers. But even my music doesn't settle it. I shift uncomfortably in my seat, moving closer to the window, and look outside, pretending to not be bothered.

I causally watch the people pass by. Some are alone with headphones, like how I was, some are with friends, partners and others with their families. It's strange. All of these people have their own story, their own thoughts and feelings. Everyone is just living their life. Just like I am. Everyone has family and friends, people who care and love them, but I'll never know them. I'll never know their tale, their plans, their backgrounds, their everyday thoughts.

It's all being told. But not here.

Once I finish my drink, I wrap up my sandwich in a napkin, pay and leave a generous tip then start walking again. But this time, I have this strange, unsettling feeling. I don't do anything about it, but no matter how hard I try to block it out, it doesn't go away.
I spend my walk constantly checking behind me. Just in case. But get distracted by a small book shop across from a small park. Maybe I could press pause on my walk and sit with a book? I mean, I'm a good few miles away from the hotel and I could do with a quick rest, I could then bring it back to finish. Besides, I haven't read a book in years. Well, not a fictional book anyway. I miss the feeling of reading, when you're so into a book it feels like you're really there, in with all of the mysteries and action. You can just be. In a completely different world.

After a quick debate I enter the shop and scan through the YA books. One book, going by the name 'Just us', catches my attention. I read the blurb and am immediately hooked. I take it over to the register and purchase it.

The cashier wishes me a good day and as soon as I exit the shop I immediately want to start reading. So I enter the park and sit on the closest bench. Sure, this isn't safe, but I won't be here for long. I'll just read and rest my feet for a little while.

But by the time I put my book down, at least 5 hours had passed. I throw back my head and groan in frustration. There is no way I've spent 5 hours reading! And not just that, but I've spent 5 hours reading nothing but fiction! Reading this book was not at all productive in any way. So I stand up and put it in my bag.

As I stand up I notice a slight chill in the air, not only that but it almost feels like there's tension surrounding me, but I'm not sure why. The sun's starting to set and everyone's started going home, giving the park a more eerie feel. I start to walk to the gate but notice a person standing beside it. It seems to be a man, but I can't see anyone else with him. Just in case I turn and start walking in the opposite direction, and while walking I seem to kick something.

Assuming I've dropped something, I bend down to look at what it was, but before I could pick it up I felt a sharp pain on the back of my head, I quickly grasped my head and fall to the floor. I can hear someone whispering behind me, but their words are muffled. I fight and try to stand up again, but the pain has spread through my entire body. I'm kicked back down and my head slams down on the concrete path. Then everything just goes black. I can't see, I can't hear nor can I think...

19.
Beginning a new

Hearing the door slam shut, my eyes start to well up.
What in the world just happened? Everything happened so fast, it all escalated so quickly...

I scan the room, reading the expressions of everyone who is left. They seem equally as stunned, confused. They're all frozen. Obviously scared to break the silence that has fallen over us. But fortunately for them, my sigh lifts the silence.

"What... what just happened?" Rose asks, Val turns to her, pulling her into a tight hug. I can't tell for sure, but something tells me she's crying. I look over at Bleu, who's sitting beside me, Their eyes are locked on the doorway. I

gentilly place my hand on their shoulder, a shiver is sent through their body, but other than that, they stay completely still.
"Bleu? Are you ok?" My voice is quiet, soft. I myself feel so many mixed emotions, but I know I'll be fine. Bleu is who I'm worried about. They surely need someone right now, and I'm always going to put them before myself.
They've been put through so much already... I don't want this to make things worse for them.
"They... they're coming back. Right? They'll be back soon?" I turn their head to face me, breaking their concentration, and loosely hug them.
"I don't think so..." I whisper, but I know they heard me.

We all stay like this for a while, Me and Val comforting our other halves, my twin and her girlfriend. Well, they haven't labelled anything yet, or confirmed anything officially. But I can see it, and I'm sure everyone else can too. Besides, now is probably not the best time to bring up said topic. But there is definitely something there. A small spark, bright and happy. It may be dimmed now, but it's still there. Still trying. still fighting. Like them. Like all of us...

"Uhm guys..." Leila's voice causes us to slowly return back to reality and focus on her. Everyone looks at her with desperation in their eyes...
"What do we do Leila?" Val questions, sounding defeated. She has her arm around Rose's waist while her head is on her shoulder. Leila sighs, hanging her head.
"I don't know. We... We can't do anything." She scratches her arm, then plays with her necklace. "They've left... we're not able to do anything... we just have to continue, go back to how we were before-"
"But how... What if what Ash said was true? What if we're all in danger! I don't think I can just move on with that knowledge." I say frantically. I know Ash has clearly proven that they aren't who I thought they were, but there is some part of me that believes them. I don't really know why, but it's hard to ignore such a strong feeling. I have to believe that there's some truth in their words... somewhere...
"Max! How could you possibly think that! After all of that?" Rose snaps, finally finding her voice. I avoid eye contact.
"Rose calm down-"
"No. Leila. I won't calm down. There's no way Ash was telling the truth! They just realised they'd been caught out and tried coming up

with a lie on the spot, which was absolutely terrible by the way." Leila goes to object but Rose cuts her off again. "Why can't you see it? It's so obvious! They aren't the person you once called a friend! Accept that and get with the program!" Then the room falls silent. So silent you could hear a pin drop. I swallow hard and look between the two sisters. Leila doesn't say anything, or go to say anything. She just stands still. Her facial expression alters, As if life was slowly being drained out of her. She looks completely black and white.
"Mum is out tonight. Your friends can all stay the night if they want. Just don't go up to the top floor." and that's the last thing we heard from her. She left and presumably went upstairs. I look at Bleu while Val tries to calm down Rose.
"Do you want to stay or go home?" they don't reply.
"Bleu?" I went to move my chair a little closer but there was no need. They stand up and immediately head for the door. I speed walked after them, calling out their name until they stopped in the main hallway, a few feet away from the door.
"I want to go home Max!" I stop a step or so behind them. They lift up a hand to their face and wipe stray tears away. I soften up.

"Ok, let's go home then. It's ok." I reply calmly, taking a step closer.
"We can't! Visiting hours are over!" My eyes widened. Then I notice more tears filling their eyes. I frown and pull them into a hug, letting them cry into my hoodie while I try not to cry myself.
"Let's stay the night… it's getting pretty dark out. But I promise we can go home tomorrow, as soon as it opens." the words taste strange, salty, kind of. Or maybe it's just my tears? Either way. Something feels off. It feels like I'm making a false promise, promising things I can't truly make happen, filling them with false hope, false positivity. But I have no choice. I can't let them slip any further…

I walk them back to the nearest seat, pass them their backpack before heading back to Rose and Val. they're still in the dining room but they're sitting down. Tears streaming down Rose's cheeks. I knock lightly on the door, to announce my presents.

"Me and Bleu are going to stay… Rose, do you know where we can sleep?" I ask in a quiet, calm voice. She wipes her cheeks and nods.
"Up the first flight of stairs, turn to your right and there are 2 spare bedrooms opposite the

window. You both can sleep in those, Val can sleep on my sofa bed." while she talks I look over to Bleu through the door, their playing with a charm on the zip of their bag, I nod.
"Thank you. uhm we're going to head up now, Bleu's really tired." I say, not looking at her. She says something but I was only half listening. Once the noise from her direction stops I hum something and then try to get Bleu's attention. I guided them to the rooms Rose was talking about, helped them get settled, then got myself ready. My mind is spinning the entire time. There's so many different thoughts but I'm eventually able to split them into two groups. On one hand, I want to believe this is all some crazy, messed up dream. A dream that Me and Ash can laugh over tomorrow. But on the other hand, I know, deep down, that the others are right. That Ash isn't the person I thought they were. That this is all real life and I can't keep hiding myself from the truth, or keep denying it.
As I climb into the unfamiliar bed I decide that I'm not sleeping tonight. I look up at the ceiling, thinking of nothing. How can I? Up until this point my thoughts have just been betraying me. A huge lie to stop me or others from frowning.
I can't trust my own mind.

"Max... I... I can't sleep." Bleu's voice snaps me out of my slump. I sit up, move to the side and tap on the spot beside me. Gesturing for them to sit next to me.
"Neither can I." I responded. They take the space beside me, bringing their knees up to their chest. I put my hand on their shoulder.
"I miss Ash... They were one of my favourite people..." They sob quietly. A sigh escapes my lips.
"I know... But you know Ash isn't who they said they are? Right?" I ask simply, I try to move closer to them but they turn their head in the opposite direction.
"But how do we know?" I raise an eyebrow.
"What?"
"How do we know? We don't. There's no actual proof that they were lying or telling the truth.. We're all just making assumptions during a really tense moment. None of us can really fully trust anything anyone said if you think about it." they explain. For a moment I'm confused, but then I start to understand.
"I guess you're right... but they've run off. None of us know where they've gone, and we can't just drop everything and run around after them completely clueless." I try to give them a hug but they push me away, so I stay back.

"Whatever. I'm going to bed." I don't stop them. I just watch them storm off and slam the door behind them, completely blank faced.

I flop back on the bed, sinking into it. Nothing today is making any sense. Why can't everything just go back to how it was yesterday?

20.
Everything's a mess!

I wake up to my name being called throughout the house. Though, I don't answer anyone. I turn on my side, but I don't fall asleep. I just look around the room. It's not exactly messy, but It's definitely not clean. They left in such a hurry... almost everything is still here. Stuff from their favourite hoodie to their stuffed elephant. I'd like to think they'd come back for them, maybe then I'd be able to convince them to stay. But then again, they don't care about me, not the same way I care about them. They only care about what the others think, what they see them as. My opinion is invalid. They made that very clear.

"Leila?" there's my name again... I don't reply, instead I wait for the front door to open and

close and then get up. I don't want to see anyone right now. I eventually find the energy to get up and walk into the bathroom. But I stop as soon as I push open the door. The imagine in front of me stopping me dead in my tracks. The room is completely burnt! My hands cover my mouth as I look around. What in the world happened here? What could have possibly caused all of this? And how didn't I know!
I consider leaving but something on the floor catches my attention. Mainly because it's not burnt? I carefully approach it, picking it up and examining it. It's a photo frame. And, aside from the cracks in the glass, it's completely unharmed. Which is surprising since every single little thing in this room is completely scorched or now a pile of ashes. I turn it around and look at the photo.
It's a picture of... us?
It's a picture of me, Ash, Rose, Alex and our parents. A single tear starts to roll freely down my cheek and onto the frame. It was taken outside of a holiday park. Me and Ash are holding up our comfort teddies, Which causes me to look back at the stuffed elephant on the bed, then back to the photo. It's pretty dirty but other than that, it looks the exact same. I never knew they'd kept it. I unfortunately threw mine a few years ago...

I continue looking at the photo. Rose was on my dad's shoulders, my mum beside them. Ash's parents were standing closer to the camera, Ash's dad being the one with the selfie stick. I remember him loving it alot. And Alex… He is crouched down in front of me and Ash, obviously trying to get in our way while also posing for the camera. It almost makes me laugh as the memories of the day start flowing back to me. But seeing his face gives me a strange feeling. I barely recognise him, as if he was a stranger. But we all look very different here, it's probably nothing, but I can't help but feel slightly off at the sight of him.

I take a slow walk back into the bedroom, placing the frame on the desk and heading for the closet. Most of their clothes that we'd brought are still here. They really didn't take much at all. Maybe that shouldn't be something to worry over, but I can't help it.
I take an oversized hoodie and chuck it on over my pyjamas since I can't be bothered to go into my own room. But it's fine, I'm home alone. Everyone is either working or at school, just like usual. No one is around to pick up on my choice of clothing.

For the rest of the day, I mostly chill around the house, doing some cleaning and revision every now and again but nothing too big. Now when I read the clock it tells me it's just passed half 5. Wow, time really does fly when you're not paying attention. My mom is still out, probably working late or out with her work colleagues, and Rose is most likely with Val, meaning both of them won't be back for a while. I'd like to say I've gotten used to being alone, but I'd be lying. When I start to get restless I head up to my bedroom and pick out some proper clothes. A white top and brown cargo's should do. I'm only planning on going on a quick walk. So I head to my bathroom, but I accidentally kick something on my way. It moves and I jump back with a loud scream.

"Ouch girl! I know I'm small but wow! Watch where you're stepping!" I hide behind my wardrobe, poking my head around it and looking down. I then see a small black kitten looking up at me. And, wait. did it just… talk?
"Y… you. you just talked!" I stammer, peering further around. I must be going crazy! Obviously. cat's don't just talk to you!
"Yes yes. I can talk, but that's really not important, don't think too much about it. I need

your help." It's voice is more serious now. I just start laughing.
"Wow. It took me a while, but I've finally snapped. Fun. I'm going to bed." I declare, stepping out from my hiding spot to head for my bed. I place my hand on my forehead and groan. What in the world? I close my eyes and take a few deep breaths, hoping this cat disappears, but when I open my eyes again, It's sitting on my bed, staring up at me. I scream again. I look between where it is and where it was with a raised eyebrow. There is no way it got that far without making a single sound?
"I'm magic. Idiot." ok, I should have expected that. I sigh, sitting beside it and crossing my legs.
"Ok, Magical talking cat, why are you here? And why in the world are you talking to me?" I ask, feeling nothing but stupidity. I'm talking to a bloody cat! Who is now pointing its paw at me.
"Normally, you wouldn't be able to understand me. But I pulled some strings so you could help me." I chuckle, using my finger to put its paw down.
"And what can I do exactly? I don't know if you know this but, uh, me and my magic are pretty useless for, well, everything. Like, look where I

am right now." I joke, but I'm only laughing on the outside. I have gotten absolutely nowhere, I spend my days roaming my house, I'm nowhere near where I wanted to be. I'm a stranger to my own friends and family, let alone the entire world!

"I wouldn't say you're useless. And if it makes you feel any better, we may not even need magic… maybe." she turns her head away and I watch her ears drop.
"Ok. Well, what is it you need help with? You've not actually said." I expect it's something really simple, like they need someone with hands to grab something off a high shelf, or something huge! Like they are giving me a life threatening, death defying mission I have to complete! I mean, that's usually why random animals start talking to people on TV. and Honestly, I could use a cool mission to spruce up my life. But I know the chances of it being that are very slim.

"I need help finding Ash-" If I was drinking something right now, we'd both be wearing it.
"Wait! Hold up! Misty?"
"You didn't know it was me?" I shake my head profusely.

"Ash never told me you could talk!" I point out in shock. Then something clicks. "They didn't tell me anything..." I look down at my hands in my lap.

"Yeah well.. they only learnt that themselves not too long ago. Anyway, when we left last night we stayed in a hotel, then they left to go for a walk this morning but haven't returned... I need you and the others to help me find them." I swallow hard.

"Are you sure they didn't just leave you like they did us?" I ask, getting up from my bed. I wipe my eyes discreetly and watch her jump from my bed to my window sill.

"I'm their animal companion, their guide, I'm pretty much a part of them. I know something is wrong." I approach the glazed window, feeling slightly bad. I look out onto the fuzzy streets and think.

"Can't you, I don't know. Tap into their mind or something then? See where they are?" I ask, seriously.

"Normally I can, but I've already tried. My connection is too weak so I can't take any clear readings" I put my hand on my chin as I think. I know I don't know the new Ash, but I definitely knew the old Ash. We were inseparable as children, we knew everything about each other. I know we aren't children now, but there's still gotta be some of the old them somewhere, right? The only thing I can do is think like how younger Ash would think.

"I can't think of a reason for the weak connection. As long as they're around here in Ventura I should have no problem reaching them." I hear Misty talk to herself, but I block it out and continue thinking. And then it hits me. Familia!

"Familia! Their brother! Could they be with him?" Me and Misty both snap our heads around to each other. I smile with pride, thinking I've just solved the problem. But when I look at Misty, she doesn't seem happy, she seems more anxious?

I didn't even know a cat could look anxious until now.

"You're right. They did say about wanting to save their brother…" My smile drops. Save? "why would they need to 'save' him?" My pride is now slowly being replaced with fear. Why would Alex need saving? What does he need saving from?

"He's with those horrible people who took both him and Ash in after their parents died. you know, the ones trying to take over Ventura?" Her explanation doesn't make me any less confused, which she picks up on. "The people Ash warned you about before they left?

Weren't you also the one who told them about those rumours? Do you seriously not remember? That's why Ash has been so stressed lately-" So Ash was telling the truth..? There really is an organisation trying to take over the island... And they have Alex! And possibly Ash too! I dart over to my wardrobe and start rummaging through it.
"What are you doing?" Misty asks me as I throw my clothes onto my floor, trying to find something.
"Ash is in trouble! As is the entire island! And I'm going to help them!" Eventually I found what I was looking for. A small but long wooden box. I remove it from its hiding place, open it up and reveal my most prized possession. My dads wand...
"Wait... how'd you get a wand?" she asks while I examine it, making sure it's still in good conditions. It's been tucked behind here for a pretty long time.
"It was my dads, he gave it to me before he died. I've always wanted to become famous, to be noticed. I wanted to master the 4 main elements. But I gave up. So I hid it away. But this is important, It'll give us an extra boost of magic on our side." I explain, finally getting into the clothes I'd picked out earlier. I may not

have trained with it for long, but I know the basics.

"Well that's great! But we're gonna need the others too." Misty jumps down and starts following me around my room. I grab a backpack, chuck in basic essentials and throw it over my shoulder.

"Well we're just going to have to convince them to help us then aren't we? Let's go!" I'm not wasting anymore time. I've got to convince the others to help me, then we've got to create a plan and actually carry it out! I can't stand around any longer. Ash is in trouble and the quicker we save them the less those horrible people can do to them.

Misty jumps up onto my opposite shoulder and points her paw forward.

"Lead the way amiga!"

21.
Got a mission

Before leaving the house I wrote a quick note to my mom. Nothing too special, since she probably won't even read it. It says that I'm staying over at a friend's place for a few nights and Rose might come with me. Once I've found some blu tack and stuck it to the wall, me and Misty set out to find the others. Fortunately, Val's house isn't too far. Rose should be over there. But just to check I pull out my phone and look for her contact, calling her as soon as I find it.

"Hey, Leila?" I hear her squeak down the phone. Her signal must not be great, meaning she's most likely outside.

"Hey, are you still with Val? I need to talk to you both." I say with a more serious tone, her's changes as well.

"Uh yeah. We're actually walking back now. Why? What do you need to talk to us about?" I notice the worry in her voice but don't go to explain. I feel like I need to tell them in person, so I keep it brief.

"I'd rather say face to face. Can you guys meet me at the park on the corner of our road? It should be quiet there."

"Yeah, that's fine. But what-" I hung up the phone then, cutting her questioning short. I can answer her questions at the park.

Looking up at the sky, I notice how dark it's gotten. I'm praying they agree to help me, and that they know where we can stay. This will no doubt take more than one evening and we can't risk nosy parents over hearing anything and getting in the way. Also, this could very easily take a turn for the worst, which is very likely, so we need a secure place to hide out in case that happens. But whether or not we have a hide out doesn't matter if we don't even have a plan! We probably can find a place to stay but then fail to come up with a plan in time! But then-

"Woah, Leila? Why are you so stressed? You could feel the tension from the other side of the damn island!" Misty's questions made me jump, I forgot about that factor. I try to calm myself down.
"Because. I'm about to walk up to my sister and her friend and say 'oh yeah, so I know you're all still on edge about everything that happened last night with Ash, and so am I, but their cat told me that they were telling the truth and have possibly been kidnapped by the organisation they told us about and now we have to go help them." I say in a sped up, higher pitched, mocking voice, adding air quotes here and there, laughing awkwardly afterwards.
"You'll be fine. If the worst comes to worst, we go alone." Her reassurance fails miserably.
"And what makes you think going alone would work! Like I told you before, My magic is useless!" I groan, turning my head away.
"And I've already said how I very much doubt that statement. Anyway- oh, there's your sister and Val!" I notice we're getting closer to the park so drop the topic. Val waves me over to her as soon as she notices my presence. Rose just stands there, looking clearly unsettled. I bet she's seen Misty-

"Hey Leila, what do you need?" Val asks simply, guiding us all to the nearest bench. I sigh, preparing myself.

"I know you guys uh-"

"It's about Ash. Isn't it?" Rose interrupts. I look over at her sadly, nodding.

"How did you know that?" Val's eyebrows raise.

"Misty, the cat on Leila's shoulder. She's Ash's pet." Her voice is sharp. She's put her walls up, I can tell.

"Hey I'm not just a pet!" I laugh as Misty tries to defend herself. But both Val and Rose just look at me, clearly thinking I'm going crazy. Oh. right. They can't hear her.

"Oh, yeah. Misty's not just their pet. She just said" I try to explain, but only Rose seems to understand.

"If she's magical that means she's their companion."

"Wait- how did you know that?"

"My old friend Rebecca had one?" My mouth falls open.

"She did?"

"Yeah, did you not know? Anyway, Ash having one doesn't make any sense, since they are only assigned to more powerful witches, and Ash doesn't have any magical ability." She leans in, inspecting Misty, who has now jumped down to hide behind me.

"Ash definitely isn't powerless." Misty tells me. I sigh, putting a hand on my forehead.

"She says Ash does have magic-" I repeat. "Don't you remember when… uh-"

"Yeah. I remember…" Val cuts in, shivering. Rose rolls her eyes.

"Ok. whatever. That's not important right now." I rise from the bench, picking up Misty again. "You're right, It's not. Misty came to me and told me Ash was in trouble. What they said last night was true. There is an organisation out there, trying to take over our island, and they've got Ash, and their brother." I say assertively, trying to stand tall. They both look at each other, then back at me, folding their arms.

"Leila, I get it. They're your best friend. But you can't believe them, or their pet." Rose gets up and tries to put a hand on my shoulder, but I push her hand away.

"No. I can. Because they're my best friend that means I know them better than you all! And I believe that they are telling the truth! And I'm going to help them, whether you join me or not. So, are you in or out?" My anger takes over me and my expressions, It surprises me so I push it back down. Neither of them respond to me

straight away. They look into each other's eyes for a while, as if they were communicating telepathically. I wait impatiently.
"Fine. but only because you're so insistent. There's no way I'll forgive them for what they did though. Not until we get a genuine apology at least." I nod as Rose talks. I'm not asking for them to forgive them, I'm asking they believe and trust me. Our friend and home are in danger and I need all hands on deck.

"I'll text Max and Bleu. there at the hospital a few blocks away. If they want to join us we can talk and come up with a plan." Val says, pulling out her phone. Me and Rose agree and we all start walking towards the hospital. Val walks slightly faster, meaning me and Rose fall behind. I'm assuming she gets tired of the silence because she breaks it quite quickly.

"I hope your right sis, as much as I don't want to jump into a life threatening mission, I want to know Ash was telling the truth…" She speaks in a quiet whisper but I can still hear her. The streets around this time are quite quiet after all. I pull her into a side hug.
"Trust me, Ash was telling the truth. Sure, they definitely didn't go about this all in the right way, but their intention was good. They must

not have known any other way of dealing with this situation. You know, Ash was always coming up with solutions for problems quite quickly as a kid. They were quick, but not necessarily 'the best'. I'm sure that's what they've done here. It is a pretty big burden to carry around too." I explain, and a small smile tugs at her lips. I smile softly.
"And don't worry. Me and dad will protect you." I add in an extra attempt to reassure her. I won't let anything happen to her. She's my little sister, the only family member I have left.

Although I'm not quite sure how Ash found out about everything, they did, and I don't blame them for hiding it until they were ready. I can't imagine how I'd cope with such a secret. I don't even know where I'd start with anything! As much as I wish they'd asked for help, I'm starting to understand why they didn't.

"Thank you- wait. You and dad? What do you mean?"
"Alright guys were close, according to Max they're down that road. They've already agreed to help us." I ignore Rose's questions and catch up to Val, as does she. I see Max and Bleu running towards us from the other street. We all meet on the corner and greet one

another, then I turn to Misty, who was once again sitting on my right shoulder.

"Ok Misty. Where to now?" I ask proudly, taking charge. Misty thinks for a while before answering, giving Val time to explain to the twins why I'm talking to a cat.

"Well there's no actual report of anyone invading any towns or villages as of yet. They must have a base set up somewhere, somewhere originally uninhabited and big enough to hold such a place." she starts, I repeat what she says to the others who all nod in unison.

"The only spot on the island that is big enough for a base and that is originally inhabited is Bosque Vacío." Val explains, looking up from her phone screen.

"Bosque what?" Bleu asks curiously.

"Bosque Vacío. It's the biggest abandoned forest in Ventura. It was left untouched on purpose to leave a home for the wildlife." Rose explains simply, Bleu nods as they start to understand.

"That would make sense, since the forest is so out of reach it would be the perfect place for a secret base, and it's right on the edge of the island. That's probably why my connection to Ash is so weak. Since the island's magic source is in the centre of the island, the further away you are, the weaker most abilities become." I once again repeat what Misty says to the others.

"Hold up... if our magic gets weaker the further away we get, how are we going to free Ash?" Max asks. I can hear the immediate worry in his voice.

"Our magic will still work if we're still on the island's soil, but would become a lot weaker. It doesn't mean our magic won't work but it'll take a lot more energy to use." Rose sighs. I forgot she takes extra history classes. And I always said that they were a waste of time.

"I think I know how to get there. But we can't get there tonight. It's at least a 28 hour walk in total. We need a place to stay." Val says. Apparently one of her moms was an adventurer, she has all her old maps up in their attic. "I can grab the map in the morning, she always goes out with her friends for breakfast before work." We all nod.

"Ok then. Now we just need a place to stay. It's getting late and we can't afford any of our parents finding out." I threw in, resting a hand on my cheek. Max nervously steps in.

"We can stay at ours... our mum won't be home..." His voice sounds shaky. We all look at each other, then collectively agree that that's the best option. Bleu then leads the way to their house. Max walks behind everyone, and once I notice, I go to check if he's ok.

"Hey bud, are you ok?" I ask in a soft tone. I'm not going to let his fear go unnoticed.
"Uhm, yeah. I'm just worried… we're about to walk into a very dangerous place with pretty dangerous people." He confesses with a low head.
"Don't worry Max, like I said to Rose, we'll be ok. I won't let anything bad happen to you. And as soon as we free Ash, we'll be unbeatable!" He laughs while I pull a superhero pose. I smile sweetly.
"Are you sure?"
"I'm sure. Trust me"

Honestly, I'm not sure, but I know that everything will become easier with Ash here. They've always been better at leading and taking charge. With them we'll be much better off. But either way, nothing too bad can happen to us.

Right?

22.
I'm sorry.

I wake up with a raging head, grasping it with one hand I use the other to help myself up. My vision is the last sense that returns. But I don't need my vision to know I'm not at the park anymore. The floor is cold and very clearly metal, the walls feel rustic and are seemingly quite tall. I slowly try to get back on my feet, falling the first few times, but eventually succeeding. As soon as I can see fully I try to figure out where I am. It doesn't take too long, the large metal bars on one side of the room give it away. I walk up to them and wrap my hands around two poles, scanning the corridor outside. At first everything is a big mystery, until a few guards walk past wearing a familiar uniform, with an extremely familiar symbol plastered on every piece of clothing.

They've found me...

I try calling out to one of the guards, I don't get their attention straight away, but after purposely being annoying for a good few minutes, one of them finally approaches my cell.

"What do you want?" she asks seriously. I try to remember her face but I can't place her name. She must be from a different department, and I need to figure out which one so I know where I am.
"What department are you from? I don't recognise you." I try to seem calm, like I know exactly what I'm doing. Confidence is key, afterall.
"Uh- department 4C? Why?" woah. That was easy.

Right. I'm 5 departments away from my old one. Possibly nearer the end of the row, considering how far away she was to begin with, and these rows tend to be around 10 cells long. So worst case I'm in number 8 or 9. So going right is my best option once I'm outta here. Better than walking past more potentially occupied cells. That would mean I could be ratted out easier, but I'd have to go through more back corridors. Maybe I can try getting myself moved. I mean, what harm could trying do? I'm already trapped. Kind of running out or worse, worse case scenarios.

"Ahem. Why do you ask?" she pretends to cough to get my attention back.
"Oh. right. Well, Mr Hatchett actually came in, I heard him tell another guard that I should be moved. I think he said 3B?" I check over my nails as I talk, still acting.
"Mr Hatchett? But I was just-" My smile grows then dies down when I hear another voice cut her off. Both me and the guard freeze. Oh no.

"Rebbeca? Why are you talking with the prisoner?" Miss Wicker... I could recognize that scratchy old voice anywhere.
"I- I'm sorry Miss Wicker... I was just leaving. Yep. just leaving." she stutters before running the opposite way down the hall. Ok, so maybe I'm in 6 or 7?
"Oh... look at what we have here. Ashley spring. My prized recruit." I narrow my eyes as she comes into view, backing away from the bars a little.
"Prized recruit? Please. Don't lie. We both know I was anything less than a decent recruit

to you." I say with a chuckle. Leaning against the wall. Feeling something like confidence. cockiness? Maybe.
"Careful Ashley. Your brother's not around to protect you now." My eyes widened. Alex... I want to cave but don't, I shake my head and try to maintain my cool.
"That's why you put me in a completely different department isn't it? No worries. I've grown up. I can handle myself." she glares at me before laughing. I start finding it harder and harder to pretend.
"If you could handle yourself you wouldn't be in a cell! But that's ok. You'll grow up someday." my blood immediately starts to boil but I don't realise how angry I am until the room starts getting brighter. My eye is glowing again. I try to calm myself down and cover my eye with my hair before she notices anything, I seem to play it off well.

"And what have you done with yourself? Honestly, when they brought you in I thought it was the wrong girl, your hair looks like it's been hacked off with kitchen scissors!" I grab the ends of my hair and examine my messy excuse for a haircut. Yes. I could've gone to an actual hairdresser and have it done properly, but I didn't want to wait anymore. Besides, I

kinda like it. It fits my style, My personality.
"And those clothes. Where were you living? Clearly nowhere with decent taste." she folds her arms as I drop mine. My posture is failing me.
"I like the way I look. And that's all that matters." my voice starts to shake but I try my hardest to not let it show.
"Is that what your precious mami told you? Before she died, that is. Oh poor child." Her words start flying towards me, like pebbles at the ocean, each hit breaking holes in my wall, which is now starting to crumble. "It's ok dear, we'll find you a new uniform, grow out your hair and forget this ever happened. Hm?" I rub my arm and look down at the floor, thinking of how much I hate myself, how much I hate how easily I'm broken down. I guess I try… that's something. But at some point, I'm always kicked back down. I sit down and lean against the wall.
"Rest up Ashley. We'll fix you tomorrow morning." she instructs before walking off. I look up at the ceiling. Completely defeated. Completely exhausted. I raise my knees to my chest and rest my head on top.

I failed.

I ran away and got picked up a while later. I'm like a money spider, I think I'm free, I think I'm finally safe, but in reality I was just delaying my fate. I can't escape. They know me too well.
I tried to be someone else, but I'm not. I'm just Ashley. Alex's quiet younger sister. The scapegoat. The minor piece left of their gigantic puzzle. The dark shadow of my team. I'm nothing, not really. It was all in my head. A small fantasy. A silly little dream. Me? A leader? No. I'm simply just their follower.
I watch as the daylight fades, the sun being replaced by the moon, I should get used to this. A life of darkness. The invasion starts in a few days, It's like what? The 2nd? The 3rd? And once they take over no light will be seen in Ventura ever again. and I'll be, once again, the blame…

"Ash?" I hear a voice but I refuse to move. My mind is good at playing tricks on me.
"Ash? Ash! There you are!" The sound of someone grabbing the bars, however, gets my attention. I turn my head, and see the last person I expected to see. I stand up.
"L- Leila?"
"Hey! Oh my god, I am so glad you're ok!" She exclaims with a bright smile. My mouth wants to fall open from shock, and I want to cry with

relief, but I don't. I pull myself together, forcing a serious expression.

"What are you doing? You shouldn't be here!" I say in a stern whisper, knowing guards will be patrolling this area like hawks. I pick up my pieces and rebuild my confident exterior. Why is she here? Last time I checked everyone hated me.

"I'm here to help you out, silly!" I fold my arms as a certain black cat jumps onto her shoulder. I sigh and look down.

"I asked her to help me. I knew something was up when you didn't come back to the hotel, I would've tried finding you myself but my connection to you was too weak." Misty explains. I sigh.

"Is that really such a bad thing?" I mutter to myself. "I thought everyone hated me? You know. I left because you were all scared of me or whatever." I clarify in a bold tone. Leila shakes her head.

"I never hated you Ash! And I tried to tell you that. Yes, the others were a little hurt, but they never hated you either. You're their friend! You're my best friend… I don't think I could ever hate you." She speaks with a sweet smile, I continue looking at her with a straight face, but inside I'm confused. They cared about me enough to come and save me? That doesn't make any sense. Seeing as they didn't even believe me a day or so ago. I thought once I'd left they'd forget about me and move on. I thought that's just how that worked? I guess not...

As Leila speaks I seem to realise something, something that I probably should have realised sooner. I fail to stop a smile from forming on my lips.

"Ok. so. How do we get you out?" she murmurs to herself with her hand on her chin. I go to say something but am cut off by a different voice.

"Here! I found these keys by the door with a few guards outside." Leila then catches a chain full of keys and the person comes into view. Rose!

"Oh my god! Rose?" I say in another loud whisper. She turns to me, pauses, then smirks.

"Hey Ash. Seem to have gotten yourself in a little situation huh?" We both chuckle, watching Leila fumble with the bunch of keys, trying to find the right one.

Eventually she finds the right one, pushes the bars to the side and runs into my cell, immediately pulling me into a tight hug. I stand still with a weak smile, tapping her on the back a few times, Then pull away.

"Ugh finally! That cell really wasn't the most comfortable of places. I can't wait to get back." I stretch and sigh with relief. Misty jumps back onto my shoulder and I immediately start feeling more like myself. I walk out of the cell, leaving Leila standing behind me. Rose and I then share a quick hug before we decide to make a move.

"We should go before the guards come back, the checks are usually hourly, but I wouldn't be surprised if they'd changed the schedule after I left"

"Wait. what do you mean after you left?" Rose asks. Oh. right. That.

"This is where I've been for the past 6 years-"

"What?" Leila shouts a little too loudly.

"Yeah. now you've probably woken up any nearby guards, so we better get going. I'll explain later." we all nod at each other and start making our way outside, Rose tells me where the others are so I know where to head for. I obviously take the lead as we walk, guiding them through the back corridors. These corridors don't tend to have as many cameras or guards patrolling them, since they don't go anywhere practically interesting. I also know where all the exits are. Rose asks me how I know the layout so well, and I remind her I've grown up in these halls and taught myself how

to get from one place to another without being spotted. I then had to silence the conversation when I spotted a guard looking in our direction, thankfully we hid just in time and weren't caught. Once the coast was clear again I gestured for the other two to keep following me. Within the next few minutes we reach the right exit and make our way into the courtyard, but we aren't fully in the clear until we pass through the back gates.
As soon as we were in view of the others Bleu runs up and gives me a big hug, I hug them back and laugh.

"Hey Bleu!"
"Hey Ash! I missed you so much!" They hug me even tighter and I dramatically gasp for air, causing Max to laugh and pull Bleu back, giving me space. I thanked him while giving him a high five. Then I turn to Val... my smile falters as I hold out my hand.
"Hey... uh-" she stares at me, her arms folded, as if she's expecting me to say something. I close my eyes and take a deep breath. Here it goes. I owe them this at the least. "Look... I'm sorry. There. I- I'm truly sorry. I really am." I look down at the ground, kicking stones while I talk. Eye contact in serious situations isn't one of my strong points, neither are apologies, but

they deserve one. A genuine one. I take a glance back up at them and they're all looking at me with soft eyes.

"Look, Ash," Val starts, taking a step towards me. "You're a good person. I wouldn't be here if you weren't. I know you've got a pure heart, and good intentions. Somewhere. And we shouldn't have pounced on you like that. But I'm sure you know, how you did what you did was not the best way to go about it. And it'll take time to rebuild the same type of connection we had before, but I know they'll forgive you soon enough, as will I. After all, you were nothing but the best to us up until this point. I think I speak for everyone here when I say you picked us all up, helped us out of the dark. And that's not easy to do, especially for one person alone. Your heart was in the right place, it was just a little full. overwhelmed." Her words cause tears to build up in my eyes. She isn't quite smiling but I can see she's not angry. She's holding her ground and being honest with me, which I respect. I appreciate her words.

"I've been stuck up here for years and the entire time I was left to fend for myself, I had to trust myself and myself only. Because the people I did trust stabbed me in the back when I least expected it. I grew up knowing that if I didn't protect myself, no one else would. I never really had friends… only family. And that was my normal, that's just how I thought they were supposed to be. But- I think I've finally realised that that's not true…" I wipe a stray tear from my eye. "I don't expect your trust and forgiveness right away. Heck, I don't deserve it. But I promise you, from now on, I'll try and unlearn these traits. I'll try to be more open with you guys. Because… you're my friends… I… I know what that word means now…" I make sure I come across as genuine, because I am. I mean everything I said.

Maybe it'll take me a while to forget a few things, but I know that and I'm ready to start trying. I completely forgot how to be a true friend, and they deserve to know that. I may have been good at it when I was younger. But that was so long ago. I hate how quickly I was changed, but I was young. I guess I can't hold that against myself forever. It's not like I can go back and tell my younger self not to change, or to do something different.
We start our walk back but something clicks. Something stops me dead in my tracks, freezing me in place. Something? Or rather someone.

"Alex!" I suddenly shout, grasping my head and looking down. Everyone stops and turns to me, confusion shared among them.

I forgot him…

23.
Not anymore.

"Who? Ash, Are you ok?" Max asks me, concern evident. They all stop walking and look in my direction while Leila runs over to me, placing a hand on my back.
"Alex! My- My brother! He- he's still in there…" I cry, shaking profusely. I turn my head, looking over at the base. We aren't that far. We could probably get there and back before the sun rises. We have at least 2 hours, maybe a little more? "We have to go back for him!"
"Ash. I'm not sure if we can. I mean, we barely got you out-" Val sighs, but I don't listen.
"He's my brother! I- I can't just leave him. Not again!" I brush Leila's hand off and step back.
"I know but-"
"Val. he's the only one I have left… he's familia. I promised him I'd return for him… I can't break that!" I clasp together my hands as I plead. She takes a step back, scratching at her neck, clearly thinking. I turn to Rose and

the twins. Rose looks like she's also thinking, but Max and Bleu are looking at each other.
"We... we should try..." Max then speaks up. I smile, but the others just seem shocked. "He's their brother guys... I understand why they'd want to go back. He's their family, and the only one they have left. And if it were Bleu back there, I'd want to go back too... nothing is more important than family." he explains quietly.
"If it were Rose, I'd also want to go back..." Leila adds. She speaks in such a whisper that I can barely hear. I go over to Max and pull him into a quick hug.
"You- you know what it's like. You'd do anything for Bleu. just like I'd do anything for Alex... you understand." he nods with a soft smile. I step back and look at Val, as does everyone else, waiting for her approval. I can't do this without everyone's approval.
"Ugh! Fine! But we have to be super quick." she finally gives in. my vision goes blurry as I pull her into a big hug, thanking her over and over. Then we immediately get to planning an entry, since we're running dangerously low on time.

Within the next few minutes we've written out a basic rescue mission, and started carrying it out. We agreed for me and Rose to go in, since

the lower the number of people the lower the chance of being spotted becomes. So I will run in, find Alex, while Rose covers for me.
We start making our way and I sneak us around to my old department, feeling something like nostalgia once we get there.

"Right. We're here. This should still be his room, I doubt they'd have moved him." I announce quietly, pointing at a door with a silver plaque reading 'department 3B. main captain quarters'. Yes. My brother is in fact in charge of this department. He really has been everyone's favourite from the very beginning.
"Woah, Main captains quarters? Are you sure he wants to leave?" Rose jokes with a laugh, but I didn't join in. I turn my head and my expression makes her stop. She apologies and then I tell her to wait outside while I go in. she agrees, then disappears. I approach the door, knock twice, then wait impatiently for a response. He calls for whoever is outside to come in, so I look either side of me, grab a branded jacket off the hooks and walk in, hood over my head, just in case.

"Hello? Who are you and what do you want?" He has his back to the door when I enter, but he soon turns around when I don't reply. Then I

201

see him, I see his face again. And if I'm being honest… I don't recognise him.

"Hello? I asked you a question." I immediately pull down the hood. He stands up.

"W- wait? Ashley?" I smile weakly as I open my arms for a hug.

"H… hey Alex." I stammer, water filling my eyes. He pauses for a moment but eventually holds me close. My tears started to soak his jacket.

"Oh Ashley! I've missed you so much! I'd thought I'd lost you…" We both pull away and wipe away our tears. The name makes me squirm slightly but I don't say anything, I can explain that later on.

"You could never lose me. We're familia. We're all we have." I reassure him, looking up, then stepping back. He smiles but the moment quickly dies when he fully takes in my appearance.

"What in the world happened to you out there? You're a mess!" I raise an eyebrow, then look down at myself. Seriously, what's so wrong with how I look?

"Oh baby sis! I'm so sorry! Tomorrow we'll get you a brand new uniform, grow out your hair again and then you'll look just like you did before. We'll fix you in no time." That's exactly

what Miss's Wicker said... and why did they both use the words 'fix me'? The words make me shiver. I stand tall and look surprised.
"Fix me..? But I like how I look. I- I don't need... fixing?" I stutter, still in shock. I expected a comment like this from Miss Wicker, but not from him. I'm not some object that needs fixing... What's gotten into him?
"No you don't. Whoever took you clearly washed that little brain of yours. But don't worry We'll-" as I take a few steps back he takes a few steps forward.
"No. Alex. I wasn't taken! Nor brainwashed. I ran away, and I changed my look. I did all this on purpose!" I say in defence, putting my hands up.
"You ran away? Why would you do that..?"
"Because these people are evil Alex! They want to take over Ventura! They want to destroy our home! I left to help fight for the island, and I came back for you. So you can come with me and we can fight together!" I explain quickly, justifying my actions the best I can. He stops getting closer so I stop backing away. He just looks at me, His whole demeanour changing instantly.
I thought my explanation would be enough to snap him out of whatever's going on with him, but it doesn't. He just laughs. But the laugh

203

isn't the one I'm used to, it sounds completely different. My hands start trembling behind my back.
"Obviously they want to take over the island. I've known for years! And I'm happy to fight with them, I thought you'd be ok to do the same" he folds his arms across his chest.
"What? why? How are you ok with this?"
"Because, Ashley. This island may have once been my home, but it took our parents away, It almost took you away! Now I just want revenge! This place took away the people I cared about the most. Then at my lowest Miss Wicker and the others took me in! Took us both in! And they gave us a way to avenge our parents!" He seems to sound crazier with every word. I can't help but back away again, feeling slightly scared.
"I… I can't believe you right now… there is no way destroying our home is the way to avenge them! This wouldn't be what they would've wanted! Alex! We can't fight for them!" I raise my voice to hide the crack. I start to feel as though I'm getting smaller and smaller.
"Seriously? What has gotten into you! You were always on my side before!" He shouts, growing annoyed at my disobedience. I continue to shrink, My voice getting quieter and quieter, my mind telling me to cave. But my

heart is screaming something different, and the scream became louder when he raised his hand.

I don't know what it was that came over me, but something pushed me up, pulled me out of the ground. Something opened my eyes, and I realised, finally, that this isn't the first time this has happened. I was blind before, Blinded by my false views on family. But these past few weeks were enough to snap me out of that. I was so focused on keeping what was left of my biological family close, that I didn't realise how intoxicated everything between us had become. He wasn't protecting me, he was the one doing the most damage. By standing beside me but knocking me down when I got too tall. Keeping me in his pocket as a silly little token. He helped me up, taught me he was the good guy, just so I had an excuse to excuse everything else. And that's just what I did…
But I refuse to be pinned on a wall and labelled by everyone else around me, especially by him. I finally know who I am, and I will stand on my own two feet. I will pull myself off that wall and speak for myself. Because he never knew me. No one here ever did. He still thinks I'll run and hide, agree until everything goes away, but not this time. I'm not that child.

"That's because I was your little shadow!" I shout, pushing away his hand and growing taller. "For years! I did what you did for years because I had no idea how to do anything for myself! But I've changed, I've grown up! I'm my own person now. I'm not a copy of your thoughts and feelings anymore because I never was to begin with! You loved having a child to mould into a female version of you! But that's not how things work! I'm a real person! My own person! And I'm tired of having everything about me pre decided!" My confidence knocks him down, he's in shock. I watch him back away from me and assume I've won. So I calm myself down, but keep my stern tone, and hold out my hand. "And I don't want to fight against my own god damn familia! So snap out of this and leave with me!" I finished. breathing heavily. I've finally become my own person, I'm no longer some toy puppet. He needs to see that and wake up from whatever he's stuck up in!

"Get out."
"What?"
"I said get out! I don't know who you are, but you're not my sister. You're not Ashley." he points to the door and glares at me. At that

moment, something breaks. But I wouldn't say it was my heart. It was my final mask. He's right. I'm not Ashley, because she never existed. I ripped off the hoodie and shed a few tears.

"Fine. I'll leave. But, for your information. I am your sibling. The fact that you can't see that says everything. But, that's fine, because now you can't lose anything else." I don't even bother to wait for a reply. I just throw the jacket and walk out with my head held high. He doesn't get to see my break, he doesn't get the satisfaction of seeing me crumble. This was his decision. He lost me. Not the other way around. I need to remember that.

I exit the room and Rose reappears beside me, she asks me how the conversation went, and where Alex was but I don't answer. I just lead us back to the others. The sun will start rising soon, we need to hurry. Details can come after.

As soon as we're standing on safer ground questions start flying. I try to fight back my tears but quickly hit my breaking point. I collapse, dropping down to the floor, my hands and knees working at my support as my tears fall into the grass. I feel someone's hand on my back and hear the others crouching down beside me. They've stopped questioning now. But I haven't

24.
It's time

It's a long, silent walk back home. None of the others know how to say what they want to say, or ask what they want to ask, and I just don't want to talk. My thoughts are loud enough, I don't need people talking on top. In a few hours we reached the village closest to the hotel I'd stayed in. I tell the others we need to take a slight detour so I can collect my things, which we do.
The lady at the desk was trying to be difficult, but I wasn't in the mood to be respectful, so I got everything pretty easily. I know how to get my way anyway, but normally I have a filter, but the filter has a few holes today.
Since the walk home will take us around a day we decide to stay at the hideout the others had found, which is supposedly at the halfway point, for a night.
I wasn't about to complain, I desperately needed a break.
The site wasn't one of the nicest places. It's a small clearing beside a mucky looking pond

with a couple of tents scattered around, but It'll work for tonight, at least. And besides, I'm really not one with high standards when it comes to living conditions. Obviously.

"Ash, you can use this sleeping bag and there's a space in Rose and Leila's tent for you to sleep in. if that's ok?" Max asks, holding a rolled up yellow sleeping bag. I take the bag, look over at Rose and Leila and then nod.
I settle down on the left of the tent, grabbing my stuff and setting everything out. I change into my pyjamas and get ready to sleep while the others make a fire outside. The time on my phone reads 3:45pm but It's been a really long day, so I get into bed anyway.

The others are still chatting outside, they clearly think I can't hear them, but, like I said, I can hear almost everything around me 24/7. I can hear them clearly, as if they were speaking at full volume right beside me. They're talking about everything that happened today, and how they are wondering what happened between me and Alex. Hearing his name makes me tense up everytime...

But It's not just that I heard, I also heard their whispers about me...

In the morning we ate our breakfast, packed up our tents and continued our journey home. Everyone has pretty much gone back to how they were before all of this, so I don't bring up what I heard last night. They don't know I heard them after all, and I'm not about to ruin everyone's good mood. Anyway, I can't say what they said was wrong, they have every right to feel and think the way they do...
So I just spent the walk silently watching them all from behind. Rose and Val are walking ahead, while Bleu, Max and Leila are in front of me. We're pretty close to our city now. e just have to pass through these bushes and then-

"Uh, guys... you might want to see this..." Val shouts over to the rest of us. We all look at each other then run over to where she is, pushing back more branches so we can see. Just then, the sight in front of me makes my heart stop.
I hear Max and Bleu gasp and someone sniffling behind me. I scan the horrific scene, looking for a clue as to what happened, then I notice the welcome sign. The words engraved on the stone have been covered up. Now it reads

"Los calmantes del sol."

A lump gets caught in my throat as I read it out loud. I step back, as does everyone else.

"They… They've started early… Because it's definitely not the 10th yet. this doesn't make any sense! We should've had more time!" I grasp my head, my speech speeding up. We should've had more time! They've started attacking early! The plan said 10th of october! Why? why would they-

"Hey Ash. it's… it's ok. Don't worry. We'll get through this." Leila tries to reassure me that everything will be ok, but as I look around at the others, I can't believe what she is saying. She rests a hand on my shoulder, the side opposite to misty, as I drop to my knees. Everyone's just standing around, unsure of what to do now. I realise quickly that I need to be everyone's rock, so I get up, grab my notebook from my bag and start pacing.
But Leila interrupts my train of thought.

"Wait? Did you say the 10th? Of October? Isn't that your-" she tries to say 'birthday' but I cut her off.

"Yeah? But that's not important right now. We need to think up a new plan. We clearly can't go back now. We need to map out and initiate plan B." Rose tries to bring up my birthday again but I cut her off too before looking back at my notes. Why didn't I plan for this? Why didn't I create a backup plan! I should have expected something like this would've happened!

I eventually took a seat in the leaves and started writing things down, and once the others had finished questioning my choice of notebook, they helped too. I obviously ignored their questions, this is my notebook after all. I'll just rip out their pages later or something, but I'm not about to ditch everything.

"If we can't go home… where do we go?" Bleu asks carefully. I let the others figure that part out, I'm trying to figure out how much training we can crame in before the 10th, and what exactly Miss Wicker and Alex gain from invading early. The place where we sleep is the last thing I'm worried about.
"We can stay in the clearing." Leila suggests. I shut my book, stand up and sigh.
"We can't stay there. It's not hidden enough." I say to her simply. It may be out of the way but

as soon as the villages nearby get invaded we'd be toast, but then Val jumps in.
"Actually, there aren't any more places big enough for us to stay in that aren't right beside the base. I'm sure we can easily hide the clearing more. Maybe with vines and stuff?" was what she argued. Alright. She has a point.
"Ok. fine. We'll head back there but we have to go through the forest. It's too risky going through public areas now. We don't know who could spot us and give us away." Everyone nods, agreeing with me. So I put away my book and we all started walking. Well, all of us besides the twins. Who are still looking at the city.

"Guys? Are you coming?" I ask. Approaching them quietly.
"Our mom… she's all alone in that room…" Max whispers, pointing at the local hospital a few blocks down. You can see it towering over the other buildings, since it's one of the tallest structures in the entire city, and probably the island too. I put a hand on each of their shoulders.
"She'll be ok. You guys need to be strong. She's in a safe place. You know that right?" My words seem to calm them down. Either that or they're suddenly really good at pretending.

"Your right Ash…"
"You always are." We all laugh at that, catching up to the others straight after. We trail back to the clearing, it takes a good few hours but eventually we get there and set our tents back up.

It's starting to get dark so while the others are getting ready for bed me and leila go and collect firewood. We don't talk much on the way there, but on the way back we kind of have too.

We were carrying logs down past a raging stream when I tripped on a tree root, fell and grazed my legs on the rocks under the water. It was getting dark and I couldn't see the path. Now I was being pushed about by the water's current, that obviously wasn't having a good day. I try to grab onto sticks but every one that I try snaps within seconds. I begin to really panic when the water starts getting deeper and deeper.

"Ash! Hold on! I'll grab some rope!" she yells, frantically searching the area. She doesn't find any rope so uses vines instead. She creates a lasso, throws it around my chest, tightens it and starts trying to pull me closer. Meanwhile

I'm bobbing up and down, my body filling with sea water with every dunk.

Honestly, I thought I was a goner before I felt the vines tighten. Before that point I was struggling to gasp for air, trying to stop myself from drawing. But afterwards... I just gave in. I stopped trying...

I don't know what but something told me too. I guess it was... trust? So I closed my eyes and shut down my body.

I... I trusted her...

25.
Nothing left

I'm first aware of the pain in my throat, then my chest. I cough a few times, struggling to open my eyes. Then, when I can finally see, I spot a large crackling fire in front me, I'm alone too, wrapped up in my blanket on the grass. I force myself up, shivering as I do, then I look up at the sky, The smoke from the fire forming grey clouds in the otherwise clear sky. In the clear patches I see a star formation that resembles a sword.
I remember my dad showing me it as a child.

I close my eyes, remembering our last camping trip. Me and my parents watched the stars while… he looked at all the night time wildlife. My dad would tell me to spot pictures so he could draw them in his book. The sword and cat ones were my favourite. And after my mum would sing me lullabies in our little family tent. I smile at the thought, hearing their voices in my head.

I miss them…

"Hey, Ash, are you ok?" Another voice catches me off guard. I slowly open my eyes, look over my shoulder, and see Leila standing beside me. I smile weakly, on purpose.
"Hey. yeah I'm-" I cough. "I'm ok… gracias."
"Good, you were sleeping a while, I was starting to get worried." She takes a seat next to me. "Here, I made us some hot chocolate." She hands me a mug and looks up. I look at her for a minute, then back up again.
"Do you remember that one camping trip we all went on?" she asks quietly. It takes me a while but eventually I remember.
"Haha yeah! We were all roasting marshmallows and Rose burnt her mouth!" I chuckle as more memories come flooding back. Leila laughs too, to begin with, but she soon stops and clears her throat. I look back in her direction. Confused.
"What's up?" I pause. "Are you ok?" My voice is soft. I'm genuinely curious. She looks down at her drink, avoiding my gaze.
"Uh… yeah. I uhm, I just- uh-" she starts to stutter. I place a light hand on her shoulder.
"You can tell me. I'll listen." I whisper softly.

"It's just that... I guess I just feel... stuck behind?" She turns to face me afterwards. I'm not exactly sure what she means, and she can tell. "Ever since you've been back... I feel like you haven't really noticed me. I feel like, metaphorically, I've been walking behind you... catching you from behind, I guess. I've been beside you the entire time, but you never realised. Like when I told you to stay. You didn't care... it's like you hear the others but don't hear me. As an example... I've been trying, Ash. I really have. But you've never really acknowledged me..." my eyes widened as hers began to water. It takes me a little while to reply, to try to comprehend and understand her.

I had no idea... but I guess that was the problem...

She soon breaks our eye contact by wiping her eyes and facing forwards. Now I'm left staring at her side. It takes me a little longer to move, but when I do, I lay my head on her shoulder, also looking straight on. I can't see her face, but I can tell she's shocked. I am too honest, but it feels right. So I don't move, and neither does she.

"I'm sorry... so so sorry. I know that's easy to say without truly meaning it, but I do. I do mean it. In every way I can mean it. I'd say I never realised, but that's the problem... I can't go back and fix who I was. But I promise you, I'll fix who I am. For you especially. You're my favourite person Leila..." I say the last part quieter than the rest, but I hope she still heard it. I lift my head and reconnect our gazes.
"Did... did Ash spring just show... true emotion? Did Ash spring just show their vulnerable side? Wow. I'm so honoured." she jokes, nudging me softly. I roll my eyes, laughing with her.
"Don't get used to it." I chuckle, smiling at her.
"So, your favourite person huh?" She raises an eyebrow. I nod and she pulls me into a hug. I hugged her back this time.
"Seriously. You are. I love you... and I'm so sorry I made you feel like I didn't see you. I promise, I will always see you." My voice is a soft whisper. I'm starting to get tired.
"I love you too. And thank you, I wish it didn't take you almost drowning to push us to this point, but you know." Her soft, quiet laugh comforts me. I smile at her words and close my eyes. Resting my head in her lap and falling asleep. I can only assume she fell asleep too.

The next few days were rough, but we got through it. We trained, helping one another with our magic, we laughed, we cried, talked about our families and best memories, we ate and slept, not very much, but we tried.
We train for 5 days. I'd say, honestly, that we're doing quite well. We aren't at the level I'd hoped we would be but, giving the circumstances, that's understandable.
I wonder around our little clearing, watching the others train together, smiling and giving thumbs up as I do so. But then Val calls me over, causing my smile to struggle to stay bright, but It managed.

"Hey Ash, not trying to impose on anything, but why aren't you training with us? We all know you have magic now?" her voice echoes in my head. I didn't respond right away, I couldn't. What do I say to that? Why am I not training? Why am I scared? Am I still scared?
I shake off my thoughts and smile more.
"I… I already trained. I uh- I want to help you guys instead." As soon as the words leave my mouth I regret them. I notice her face and body language change instantly. If Leila hadn't helped me, I don't think I would've gotten outta that one as easy.

I apologise, obviously, but I can't let my team know that I'm scared to use my own magic. I know I promised to tell them the truth more, but I also promised that they'd be safe. If they knew I wouldn't be using my magic because of some silly fear, that would do the opposite of reassuring them. I owe them strength. Not weakness.

But that night I did ask Misty for help. Yes, I finally accepted her help. And she told me I can aim my magic, that if I think hard about who I want to protect, they should remain unharmed. It took a few tries, and a lot of noise, but I think I was able to suss it out. I did have to go deeper into the forest though, just in case I burnt down our tents.
She taught me a few other things that night too. About emotion control, and how to channel certain noises into light but it didn't really stand out to me as much. I'm not planning on using my magic, like I'd already established. But at least now I know how not to burn things down by accident. I only asked Misty for the others' sake. I didn't want to get too overwhelmed and cook them all to crisps.
I don't want any more unnecessary blood on my hands...

Now it's the night before we plan to leave. We're all sitting around our campfire, clearly all a bit on edge. But a guitar and singing quickly broke everyone's walls. No matter what happens tomorrow. We're ready. I know we are.

26.
Good to go

"Ash! Wake up!" I slowly open my eyes and adjust to the light, then jump when I see Rose's face inches away from mine.
"Agh! Woah Rose! What's wrong?" I ask, reaching for my jacket at the end of my sleeping bag.
"Come outside. Val found something!" The urgency in her voice speeds up my pace. I chuck on my jacket and run out of the tent with her, scared of what she's found. As I exit I notice everyone's already huddled in the centre of the clearing.

"What's wrong Val?" I ask, squeezing into the huddle. Everyone turns to me.
"I was scouting the area with my drones when I realised the majority of the villages nearby had already been invaded! There's barely any left!" my heart sinks to the bottom of my stomach. Leila places a hand on my shoulder as I look at

the screen. I place mine on hers and squeeze it lightly.

"We can't get to the base, we need to pass through at least three of these villages, but we'd be spotted immediately!" Everyone begins chattering with everyone else while I stay silent, trying to come up with a solution. Because, once again, I didn't plan for this scenario.

There has to be some way we can get to the base without going through the villages. A way through the forests maybe..?

Wait...

I walk off from the group and over to the lake, immediately recognising the layout from one of my old books. We've unknowingly been staying in the same spot my ancestors stayed in. This is the clearing they camped out in before building proper homes, which means...

"Guys! Guys!" I shout, immediately grabbing everyone's attention. I make my way back over to the circle as I talk. "This is the same clearing my ancestors, the founders of Ventura, stayed in!" I announce proudly.

"So..? where are you going with this Ash?"

"That means we are close to the outskirts of Bosque Vacío," Rose points out quickly. I nod, smiling.

"How'd you know that?" Bleu asks.

"It's written in the legend that the two spring children were playing in this clearing, and they'd walked off a little too far and entered what is now known as 'Bosque Vacío'." I explain, hoping someone gets where I'm going with this.

"Wait… so if those children got lost in the forest, through the forest. That means we can get to the base through the forest too!" Leila says proudly.

"Exactly! And we know the base is close to the coast so-"

"So we can pass through the forest, follow the coastline until we get there!" Max finishes, cutting me off. I laughed, nodded, then looked over at Val. I can tell she's slightly sceptical. Or maybe worried?

Why does she seem worried?

"Uhm guys? Can you start packing everything away? You know, to take home afterwards." I ask, receiving a string of 'yes's soon after.

They all run into the tents but I quietly stop Val.

"Hey, Val? Can you come with me instead?" I ask, pointing over to the lake. She just nods and follows me around the lake and down a stream. We find a log and sit down. I thought this was the best place to sit, since it's out of the way.

"So, how are you feeling?" I question calmly, throwing small pebbles into the stream. I hear her sigh.
"I'm fine." clearly she's recoiling, avoiding talking about her true feelings. I can tell by the way she's sitting straight, looking away from me.
"Val... you and I both know you're not fine. What's up? Genuinely." It took a few tries but I eventually got her to look at me. She still had her masks on but I could see through a few cracks.
"You can talk to me. I won't judge you. I promise." She closes her eyes and looks down.
"I... I'm scared..."
"What's scaring you?"
"This. this organisation... The fighting... and the fact our homes are currently being invaded-" her hands crawl up to her head, grasping it as she speaks. "And my mom's are probably wondering where I am! They're probably so worried... I... and... And I'm worried about my

damn cat! And I just… want to go home, to go back to when everything was perfect, back to when I was oblivious… I want to go back to when there wasn't a chance of me dying!" by now she's crying and I've got my hand lightly on her back. I move closer.

"I understand how you feel, well… I don't have anyone waiting for me like you do… but I can understand why you're scared. It's a perfectly valid feeling. And I know it was hard to admit, but trust me, it's nothing to be ashamed of. I mean, we are probably about to walk into a whole damn war." I laugh softly at the last part, causing her to laugh too. I remove my hand and she looks up at me with watery eyes. "And sure, it's going to be dangerous. But I won't let you or any of the others get seriously hurt. You have my word." I raise one hand and put my other on my heart. "I swear that nothing bad will happen to any of you. I promise all of my friends will walk out safe and unharmed." I smile as I formally recite my oath. She laughs at me and then pulls me into a tight hug. I'm shocked at first, but then I hugged her back. She thanks me but I remind her she has no reason to thank me.

"You're a good friend Ash… truly." she pulls away to look me in the eyes. I awkwardly laugh.

"I doubt that. I mean, I try, but I'm not. I've done so much wrong and-"
"But have you considered all the things you've done right? I know I've given you a hard time since you've been back but… I really do appreciate you." She takes a deep breath. I raise an eyebrow. "I wasn't going to admit this but… I really look up to you. Ash. I have since I saw you on your first day of school. You were someone I'd never seen in any of my past schools, or anywhere for that matter. I saw you stand up for Max and watched everyone listen to you, and then how you were open and honest with Rose the same day. I admire how you're so… real. I guess." it only takes a few blinks to cause tears to run down my own cheeks.
"And… that's why you've been acting the way you have… because, I let you down? I showed you my true colours…" I mutter, looking at the waves crashing against the rocks.
"At the time… yeah. But seeing the way you've looked after us all, and helped us, and made sure none of our feelings went unnoticed. I think I respect you more now. I thought that you were just some villain, wearing a hero's mask. But now I know the villain was a mask, created by the stress you threw on yourself. You're a good friend, and a good person,

because you have flaws too. And I'm sure if you ask any of the others, they'd say the same."

Now it's my turn to hug her. I never realised how much I needed her validation until now… Ever since that moment outside the base, I'd been doubting myself. I've been putting myself down because I didn't believe I deserved their friendship, that I didn't deserve anything at all…
Because to me, I was still that little girl existing in the shadows of everyone else around me. I knew I should be in my own ray of light, but I never truly thought I deserved it… but now, after this, I finally feel like I do.
I know I deserve this. I deserve a happy ending. I deserve MY own happy ending.

"Thank you… I needed that…"

27.
Safe at last?

Me and Val walk back, maybe as different people. I don't know about her, but I definitely feel different. I feel more comfortable with myself.
The others rush over to us with confused yet relieved expressions plastered across all of their faces.

"Where did you go?"
"We thought you'd gotten lost!"
"Or that you'd fallen into the lake!" I laugh softly, glancing over at Val. Something tells me she doesn't want them to know what we were talking about, so I politely brush the others off. "We were just checking the area, making sure we'd not left anything out of place. You didn't need to worry." When Val mouths 'thank you' from across the clearing soon after, I know I've done my job.

Now I can focus on the task ahead. The mission I've been working towards for 6 years. It's finally time. And we will win. We have to win. Because if we don't... who knows what will be made of this place... we win or die trying.

"Ash? Are you sure we're ready?"
"Yes. absolutely." I hope so...

It took a good few hours of walking but we eventually reached the base. The building, unfortunately, is protected by a wall of guards. This is where Bleu and Max come in. I wave my hand at them as a signal and they're expressions immediately change. Bleu uses their telekinesis to distract half of the guards while Max calls out to a pack of wolves living nearby to distract the others. They both run their opposite ways, to make sure the guards don't return while the rest of us sneak in through some back doors. Val's tech takes out the security camera's images, and Leila freezes the cables so they snap. Just in case.

"Alright guys. Rose, I need you to help Val get into the server room. From there she can disarm any technical weapons they have stationed across the island. If there are any you can't disarm, relocate them to a safer area. And while you do that Me and Leila will scout the departments. With these earpieces," I pass around 4 earbuds. "We'll all be able to communicate with each other. We can warn you when someone is heading your way, and vice versa." they all nod in unison and I peer around the corner to check if the coast is clear. "Ok. The server room is 3 halls down. It's the only door on the right. Maybe after try to get into the communication room, we can send patrolling troops away from villages. Use 131204 if anything or anyone asks for a code. I doubt they'd have changed that. Ok. Good luck." and then we all split off.

Me and Leila spot a few guards but stay undetected. Everything seems to be going smoothly until we stumble upon… Alex…

"Ash there's a- Ash? Ash! What's wrong? You have to move otherwise-" I'm frozen in my place. Me and Alex are at opposite ends of a one way corridor. We both just… pause. 'Ash, you have to move!' I repeat to myself, but my body stays still. My mind is failing to push me out of the way. It's sending orders that my body is simply refusing. It's only when Leila

pulls me back that I snap back into my own body.
"Ash! What's wrong? You completely froze up!" I begin to stutter.
"A... A... Alex. h- he was there..." I shake, pulling on my hair before covering my face with my hands in anger. Leila moves, assuming to look down the hall, then picks me up.
"Ash, it's ok. Don't worry. But we have to move. We aren't totally safe anymore. We have to get Rose and Val." she says in an assertive tone, pulling me up out of my little mess. She helps me move until I get enough energy back to run myself. I can't worry about my stupid mistake right now. We have to get Rose and Val and get out. We can't be here while they're searching.

"Rose! Val! We need to get out! We'll have to initiate plan B after getting to safer ground! Rose? Val? Hello, are you guys there?" my heart starts to race faster as I hear Leila talk. I'm silently praying that I haven't just broken my promise... I can't lose anyone. No one will die on this mission.
I've spent so long training and planning, making sure nothing could go wrong! And I go and mess everything up!

When we reach the serve room, we see Val tinkering away while Rose is tapping her foot beside her, looking pretty anxious.

"Rose! Val! Oh my good, I'm so glad you're ok! Why didn't you answer my calls? We have to abort, we've been found out!" Me and Leila try to catch our breaths as we wait for Val to pack up. Rose claims they never heard anything through the earpiece and talks to Leila while I stand by the doorway, keeping watch.

Then I realised something.

"Guys… Guys… Guys!" I shout, shaking where I'm standing. We all turn our heads at the same time. "It's too late… they… they're here-" Just as I say it, a bunch of guards barge me out of the way of the door. As a result, I'm sent flying and hit my head on the back wall, beside the large desk. I try to stand, but keep falling. Leila notices my struggles so runs over to help me, meanwhile Val and Rose are fighting off the guards the best they can, trying hard to keep them close to the door, but they're all slowly edging closer.

"Leila! Don't worry about me! Help them! You have your wand!" I cry out, trying again to

stand up, but I've seemed to have also hit my arm on the sharp edge of the table. I hold my open wound tight.
"But you're bleeding! I can't leave you like this!"
I sigh, looking around me, looking for something to stop the bleeding. I pull off my jacket, trying my best to tie it around my wound, wincing as I tighten it.
"There. Now please, go help them…" I force a smile as she looks between me and the others. Thankfully, she eventually chooses to help them, pulling out her wand as she runs. I lean against the wall and try to contact Bleu and Max.

"Max? Bleu? Uh… our mission has been- uh… compromised. Please stay hidden…" the pain in my arm starts growing, causing my breathing to pick up its pace. " please stay safe… We'll be out with you soon. I promise…" I cut off the line as soon as I hear both of their voices, cutting out their questions. I don't want to feel any more guilt right now.

I look up at the fight in front of me, scanning every part of it. I recognise a few faces but only two stand out majorly. Alex and Miss Wicker… they're here, fighting and… going after- Leila! But she can't see them, she's distracted by the guards in front of her. I try my hardest to scream out to her, to warn her, but she can't hear me over the noise. Then I notice the other two have people secretly surrounding them too. But just like with Leila, they don't hear my cries. I immediately scan the objects around me again, hoping I can help in some way, but everything is useless! I don't have anything to use... except... no! No I can't. I'll- I'll mess it up, I'll hurt them... I... I can't risk it.

Can I?

I sigh and try screaming again, all three of them are almost completely surrounded. I have no choice. I have to... I just have to. My friends don't deserve to go this way.

I push myself up, edge closer to the fight and clutch my wounded arm. Closing my eyes and concentrating hard. Right. If I just think about who I want to help... my friends will be ok.

I feel my body growing hotter and I see the light through my eyelids. I continue to concentrate, quickly falling to my knees. I keep doing what Misty taught me, channelling the noise and chaos, taking a hold of it and using it to my advantage. The noise is my friend. It's

willing to help if I let it. Just breathe steady and don't, even for a second, take those names out of your head.
By now I'm on my hands and knees, my head hanging low. Everything feels hot, but I can't give up. No matter how much it hurts, I must finish what I've started.

I wait for myself to cool down before dropping completely to the floor. I hear muffled worried voices approaching me, so I force a small smile, feeling nothing but relief. I guess it worked…

I feel someone's soft touch on my back and Leila's voice rings in my ears. It takes me a minute or so to see again properly, but when I can, I see Rose, Val and Leila huddled in front of me, ready to help me to my feet. I thank them but they stop me.

"Thank us? No, thank you! That was awesome what you did just then!" Rose shouts in astonishment.
"Yeah! You saved us!" Val adds in a similar tone!
"You're a hero Ash! You're the reason we're alive!" I smile and grab my necklace which has fallen out of my T-shirt. I see the people who

are left crawling away behind my friends, obviously too scared to fight anymore. I sigh loudly and Rose insists on a group hug. I'm pulled into it and laugh, smiling bright and closing my eyes as our arms wrap around each other.

But just as I'm about to pull away I feel a sharp, clean pain in my back. I instinctively cry out in pain and the girls pull away in fear. My eye's lock on the door straight ahead, watching a black haired boy run out of the room, then my vision rapidly decreases. The clean line of pain spreads throughout my entire body, all while my friends are asking me the obvious questions, and holding me up as I fall forward. My vision eventually goes fully and my ears begin to fail. I just about feel my body hit the floor face first. Then... nothing...

It was like it had all flashed before my eyes; the sound, the light, the pain, the blood, the sights, the looks on my parents faces, my brother... and it was all my fault. I saw my brother's cries and my frozen expression as they announced the time of death.

I was stuck... I didn't know what to feel... or what to think... All I knew was that I was the blame, the blame that wanted nothing more than to be the reason.

And here I am… the reason… not the blame.

-acknowledgments-

How did this happen? I never would've thought that I'd be able to label FATE as finished, let alone a published novella. This has always been my biggest dream and I couldn't have done it without my family and friends. Words couldn't even begin to express how grateful I am to all of you.

Thank you to my family, my parents, my step parents, my grandparents, especially the one who is unable to read this, and my aunt. I would've given up if it wasn't for all of you. You taught me all I know, you've all helped shape me into the person I am today, and all I want is to continue to make you all proud. You're my rock. I love you all.
And thank you to my Leila, the absolute nutcase that I get to call my best friend. You mean the world to me. I love and appreciate you more than you'll ever know. I couldn't have done this without your constant support.
Even to my old school, I thank you and all those who were there during my short stay. Thank you for helping me realise that you're not what I

need. Without you, I would never have burnt out and come to the conclusion that I can build my future outside of your four walls. And to those who thought I'd be nothing without them, I would like to respectfully thank you. You were my reason for leaving after all.

After such a terrible start, I can finally tell myself that I've done it. I'm finally where I want to be and I can finally breathe.

And to those who picked up this book, I adore you. I thank you for being interested enough to pick up this copy and I love you for reading to the end. I can only hope you enjoyed reading it just as much as I enjoyed writing it. Originally I made the characters for me, so I could feel seen, but this story is for you. I hope you're able to take something away from this book and I wish you all nothing but the best.

And I guess I should apologise for the gut-wrenching ending lol <3

-Alex Phillips Hawkes-

Is a young adult author from Dorset, England. They wrote and wrote all their life, praying that one day they could share their characters with you all. There isn't one day where they can't be found spinning in their desk chair with a pen, paper and laptop in their reach. (plus, a cat or two that insist on 'helping')

They love art, music and giving the most random gifts. And they are grateful that they are able to share this gift with you.

Printed in Great Britain
by Amazon